# R Guide for Business Statistics
*Constantin Colonescu*

*2018-02-07*

Title: "R Guide for Business Statistics"

Author: Constantin Colonescu

Edmonton, Alberta

Canada

The examples presented in this book follow Black, K. (2017). *Business Statistics for Contemporary Decision Making*, Ninth Edition. Wiley.

This book has been created using the R software *bookdown* by Yihui Xie,

Xie, Y. (2016a). *bookdown: Authoring Books with R Markdown*. R package version 0.0.71.

R version: x86_64-w64-mingw32, x86_64, mingw32, x86_64, mingw32, , 3, 4.3, 2017, 11, 30, 73796, R, R version 3.4.3 (2017-11-30), Kite-Eating Tree

© 2018 Constantin Colonescu. All rights reserved.

ISBN-13: 978-1985207493

ISBN-10: 1985207494

# Contents

**1 Introduction to R**     **7**
    1.1 The RStudio Screen . . . . . . . . . . . . . . . . . . . . . . . . . 8
    1.2 Opening and Saving a File . . . . . . . . . . . . . . . . . . . . . 9
    1.3 Data Sources . . . . . . . . . . . . . . . . . . . . . . . . . . . . 12

**2 Charts and Graphs**     **15**
    2.1 Frequency Distributions . . . . . . . . . . . . . . . . . . . . . . . 15
    2.2 Quantitative Data Graphs . . . . . . . . . . . . . . . . . . . . . 17
    2.3 Qualitative Data Graphs . . . . . . . . . . . . . . . . . . . . . . 19
    2.4 Charts and Graphs for Two Variables . . . . . . . . . . . . . . . 21

**3 Descriptive Statistics**     **23**
    3.1 Measures of Central Tendency . . . . . . . . . . . . . . . . . . . 23
    3.2 Measures of Variability: Ungrouped Data . . . . . . . . . . . . . 26
    3.3 Central Tendency and Variability: Grouped Data . . . . . . . . . 29
    3.4 Measures of shape . . . . . . . . . . . . . . . . . . . . . . . . . 36
    3.5 Descriptive Statistics in R . . . . . . . . . . . . . . . . . . . . . 39

**4 Probability**     **43**

**5 Discrete Distributions**     **45**
    5.1 Statistics of a Discrete Distribution . . . . . . . . . . . . . . . . 47
    5.2 Binomial Distribution . . . . . . . . . . . . . . . . . . . . . . . . 47
    5.3 Poisson Distribution . . . . . . . . . . . . . . . . . . . . . . . . 49
    5.4 Hypergeometric Distribution . . . . . . . . . . . . . . . . . . . . 51

**6 Continuous Distributions**     **53**
    6.1 Uniform Distribution . . . . . . . . . . . . . . . . . . . . . . . . 53
    6.2 Normal Distribution . . . . . . . . . . . . . . . . . . . . . . . . 57
    6.3 Exponential Distribution . . . . . . . . . . . . . . . . . . . . . . 60

## 7 Sampling and Sampling Distributions — 63
- 7.1 Constructing a Random Sample — 63
- 7.2 Sampling Distribution of the Mean — 68
- 7.3 Sampling Distribution of the Sample Proportion — 71

## 8 Estimation for Single Populations — 73
- 8.1 Estimating the Mean with $z$-Statistic — 73
- 8.2 Estimating the Mean with $t$-Statistic — 74
- 8.3 Estimating the Population Proportion — 75
- 8.4 Estimating the Population Variance — 76
- 8.5 Determining Sample Size — 77

## 9 Hypothesis Testing: Single Populations — 81
- 9.1 Population Mean, When Variance is Known — 81
- 9.2 Population Mean, When Variance is Unknown — 82
- 9.3 Testing Hypotheses about a Proportion — 83
- 9.4 Testing Hypotheses about Variance — 84
- 9.5 Type II Errors — 85
- 9.6 Operating Characteristics and Power Curves — 88

## 10 Inferences about Two Populations — 91
- 10.1 Difference in Two Means With Known Variance — 91
- 10.2 Difference in Means with Unknown Variances — 93
- 10.3 Two Related Sample $t$-Test — 96
- 10.4 Differences in Population Proportions — 96
- 10.5 Testing Two Population Variances — 98

## 11 Analysis of Variance — 103
- 11.1 One-Way ANOVA — 103
- 11.2 The Randomized Block Design — 108
- 11.3 Two-Way ANOVA — 110

## 12 Simple Regression Analysis and Correlation — 115
- 12.1 Simple Regression Analysis — 116
- 12.2 Residual Analysis — 119
- 12.3 Standard Error of the Estimate — 120
- 12.4 Coefficient of Determination — 123
- 12.5 Hypothesis Tests in a Regression Model — 124
- 12.6 Estimation — 129
- 12.7 Forecasting Trend Line — 131
- 12.8 Interpreting the Output — 132

## 13 Multiple Regression Analysis · · · · · · · · · · · · · · · · · · · · · · · · · · · · · · · · · · · · · · · · · · · · · · · · · · · · · · · · · · 135
    13.1 Significance Tests in Multiple Regression . . . . . . . . . . . . . . . . . . . . 140
    13.2 Residuals, Stdandard Error of Estimate, and R-Squared . . . . . . . . . 143
    13.3 Interpreting Regression Output . . . . . . . . . . . . . . . . . . . . . . . . . 147

## 14 Building Regression Models · · · · · · · · · · · · · · · · · · · · · · · · · · · · · · · · · · · · · · · · · · · · · · · · · · · · · · · · · · · 149
    14.1 Nonlinear Models . . . . . . . . . . . . . . . . . . . . . . . . . . . . . . . . . . 149
    14.2 Indicator (Dummy) Variables . . . . . . . . . . . . . . . . . . . . . . . . . . 155
    14.3 Model Building: Search Procedures . . . . . . . . . . . . . . . . . . . . . . 157
    14.4 Multicollinearity . . . . . . . . . . . . . . . . . . . . . . . . . . . . . . . . . . 161
    14.5 Logistic Regression . . . . . . . . . . . . . . . . . . . . . . . . . . . . . . . . 162

## 15 Time Series Forecasting · · · · · · · · · · · · · · · · · · · · · · · · · · · · · · · · · · · · · · · · · · · · · · · · · · · · · · · · · · · · · · · · · 165
    15.1 Introduction to Forecasting . . . . . . . . . . . . . . . . . . . . . . . . . . . 165
    15.2 Smoothing Techniques . . . . . . . . . . . . . . . . . . . . . . . . . . . . . . 166
    15.3 Trend Analysis . . . . . . . . . . . . . . . . . . . . . . . . . . . . . . . . . . . 173
    15.4 Seasonal Effects . . . . . . . . . . . . . . . . . . . . . . . . . . . . . . . . . . 175
    15.5 Autocorrelation and Autoregression . . . . . . . . . . . . . . . . . . . . . 179

## 16 Analysis with Categorical Data · · · · · · · · · · · · · · · · · · · · · · · · · · · · · · · · · · · · · · · · · · · · · · · · · · · · · · 183
    16.1 Chi-Square Goodness-of-Fit Test . . . . . . . . . . . . . . . . . . . . . . . . 183
    16.2 Chi-Square Test of Independence . . . . . . . . . . . . . . . . . . . . . . . 186

## 17 Nonparametric Statistics · · · · · · · · · · · · · · · · · · · · · · · · · · · · · · · · · · · · · · · · · · · · · · · · · · · · · · · · · · · · · · · 189
    17.1 Runs Test . . . . . . . . . . . . . . . . . . . . . . . . . . . . . . . . . . . . . . 189
    17.2 Mann–Whitney U Test . . . . . . . . . . . . . . . . . . . . . . . . . . . . . . 190
    17.3 Wilcoxon Matched-Pairs Signed Rank Test . . . . . . . . . . . . . . . . . 192
    17.4 Kruskal–Wallis Test . . . . . . . . . . . . . . . . . . . . . . . . . . . . . . . . 193
    17.5 Friedman Test . . . . . . . . . . . . . . . . . . . . . . . . . . . . . . . . . . . 194
    17.6 Spearman's Rank Correlation . . . . . . . . . . . . . . . . . . . . . . . . . . 195

## 18 Statistical Quality Control · · · · · · · · · · · · · · · · · · · · · · · · · · · · · · · · · · · · · · · · · · · · · · · · · · · · · · · · · · · 197
    18.1 Control Charts . . . . . . . . . . . . . . . . . . . . . . . . . . . . . . . . . . . 197

## 19 Decision Analysis · · · · · · · · · · · · · · · · · · · · · · · · · · · · · · · · · · · · · · · · · · · · · · · · · · · · · · · · · · · · · · · · · · · · · · · · · 201
    19.1 Decision Making Under Uncertainty . . . . . . . . . . . . . . . . . . . . . . 201
    19.2 Decision Making Under Risk . . . . . . . . . . . . . . . . . . . . . . . . . . 204
    19.3 Revising Probabilities . . . . . . . . . . . . . . . . . . . . . . . . . . . . . . . 207

## References · · · · · · · · · · · · · · · · · · · · · · · · · · · · · · · · · · · · · · · · · · · · · · · · · · · · · · · · · · · · · · · · · · · · · · · · · · · · · · · · · · · · · · · 211

# Chapter 1

# Introduction to R

This *Guide* accompanies *Business Statistics for Contemporary Decision Making*, ninth edition, by Ken Black (2017). It has been written using the package bookdown (Xie 2017).

**Disclaimer**

Neither R and related packages, nor this *Guide* offer any guarantee whatsoever. Authors of these works are not responsible for any losses that might be related to the use of these materials. All material in this book is for pedagogical purposes only; various code segments may not work in all situations and shall not be used when serious consequences are possible.

R (R Core Team 2017) is open-source statistics software that can be freely downloaded at: http://www.R-project.org. The advantage of free and open-source software is, besides being free, that new developments can include parts of software that others write. Thus, an open-source system can grow much faster than a commercial one, which needs to write all its parts independently.

This *Guide* is going to use, besides R, an interface that makes the user's task easier, namely RStudio (RStudio Team 2015), which you can also download in a free version at: http://www.rstudio.com/. RStudio is all you need to see when working on a project because it will automatically use R in the background; all you need to do is to install both R and RStudio on your computer. Figure 1.1 shows the four work spaces (quadrants) of a typical RStudio screen plus various toolbars.

**Exercise**

Open RStudio, press `File` → `New File` → `R script`.

- Type `citation()` and press `Ctrl + Enter` to see how to cite R in your writings (result shows in the lower-left window).
- Type `help()` and press `Ctrl + Enter` (result shows in the lower-right window).
- Type `help(summary)`.
- Type `?summary()` and press `Ctrl+ Enter`...and I hope you have got the idea of how to use the help function. As you can see, you can either use the command `help(...)` or simply type a question mark followed by the word you want to search help for. Usually, these "words" are functions; therefore, they may need to be followed by brackets ().
- Type `# This is a comment` and press `Ctrl + Enter` to see that nothing happens. Comments are ignored by R, wherever they pop up; they can follow a command on the same line, or they stay independently on a separate line. The only function of comments is to document the script, so that you or somebody else understands the script later. Thus, they produce no effect in any window, but they will remain in the script when you save it.

## 1.1 The RStudio Screen

The first quadrant is where you write your script, which is a collection of R commands. Using a script is always advisable when solving problems, as opposed to "point-and-click" methods that other software packages provide, because a script keeps a record of all your operations and allow later reproduction of your work by yourself or others. In my experience, using well-organized scripts and documenting your steps is always the better choice. You shall save your scripts, so that you can later consult, modify, or improve them.

Scripts are text files. You can write them in any text editor, or copy them from anywhere and paste them into RStudio's first quadrant. You can also select text and move it around. To execute a line of script in this window, place the pointer on that line and press `Ctrl + Enter`; if you wish to execute several lines, select the lines and press `Ctrl + Enter`.

There is no special character for continuing a command on the next line; all you need to do is to interrupt the line such that R expects continuation, for instance after a comma, an operator, or with an unmatched bracket.

The first quadrant is also where various files open and where you can inspect your data sets. Sometimes you will work with several script files and data sets at a time you would like to be able to move back and forth among them quickly; the first quadrant makes it possible.

The second quadrant shows the "environment," which contains all the "objects" that R creates when executing your commands. The *object* is the building block of R. Data, numbers, matrices, and functions are all examples of objects that you can see and consult in the "environment" window. The second quadrant can also be turned into a "history" window showing all the commands R has executed in the current session.

In the third quadrant, you can view a list of packages (software pieces written by various authors compounding your version of R); it also gives easy access to the files on your computer and to help information; and, finally, it is where your plots appear.

Finally, the fourth quadrant is where you can see the results of your calculations. It shows both the commands that are being executed, the results, and possible errors or warnings. You can navigate through commands previously executed by using the up and down arrows on your keyboard. When R shows the ">" sign on the lower side of the quadrant, it is telling you that it is ready to execute a new command. You can type a command directly in the fourth quadrant and press Enter to execute it, but the command will be lost once you end the session.

## 1.2 Opening and Saving a File

We have already opened a new script file in the above exercise. To save it, just press File → Save As, and give it a name. To re-open it, press File → Open File...

You can keep several related files together and get quick access to them if you create an R *project*, which can be easily done using the File functionalities.

Opening data files in R is, though, a more complex issue, because it depends on where the file is and what kind of file it is. For now, suppose you have a .txt or .csv file in a directory on your computer and you would like to browse your computer in order to open it. To do this, type read.table(file.choose(), header=TRUE). Whenever you need to provide a path and file name to R, use forward slash instead of the back slash. The function read.table() can read files from the internet, when a url is provided instead of a computer path.

The function data() opens a data file that comes with an R package. Such a package has to be installed first, using the function install.packages() and then loaded into the memory with the function library(). If a package is stored at the GitHub repository (as opposed to the usual CRAN), you need to use a sequence as in the following example, which installs the package "Black9edata" and opens the file "Energy" in R.

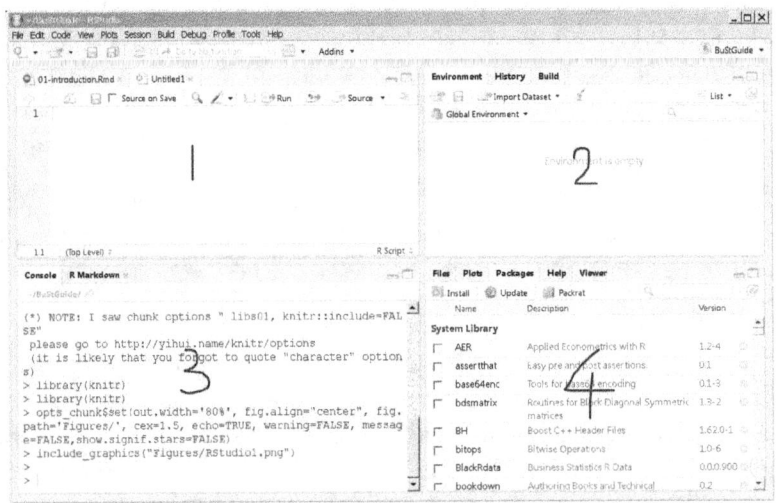

FIGURE 1.1 RStudio screen quadrants

```
# install.packages("devtools") #if not installed
library(devtools)#You need to load a package every session)
install_github("ccolonescu/Black9edata")#(if not installed yet)
library("Black9edata")
data(Energy)
```

```
library(Black9edata)
data("Energy")
head(Energy) # Shows the head of the data file
```

```
## # A tibble: 6 x 6
##    Year CrOilPrd USEnCons USNucGen USCoalPr USDryGas
##   <dbl>    <dbl>    <dbl>    <dbl>    <dbl>    <dbl>
## 1  1.00     55.7     74.3     83.5      599     21.7
## 2  2.00     55.7     72.5      114      610     20.7
## 3  3.00     52.8     70.5      172      655     19.2
## 4  4.00     57.3     74.4      191      685     19.1
## 5  5.00     59.7     76.3      251      697     19.2
## 6  6.00     60.2     78.1      276      670     19.1
```

## 1.2. OPENING AND SAVING A FILE

```
tail(Energy)  # Shows the end of the data file

## # A tibble: 6 x 6
##    Year CrOilPrd USEnCons USNucGen USCoalPr USDryGas
##    <dbl>  <dbl>   <dbl>    <dbl>   <dbl>   <dbl>
## 1  21.0   60.2    83.9     610     945     18.1
## 2  22.0   61.0    85.6     640    1034     18.8
## 3  23.0   62.3    87.2     673    1033     18.6
## 4  24.0   64.1    90.0     675    1064     18.8
## 5  25.0   66.3    90.6     629    1090     18.9
## 6  26.0   67.0    89.7     667    1110     18.9
```

Data can be entered directly from keyboard. The following code sequence demonstrates this method on the first table in Chapter 2, showing oil and coal consumption in a few countries.

```
country <- c("US", "China", "Japan", "India", "Russia","Brazil")
oilCons <- c(833.6, 461.8, 201.4, 162.3, 136.0, 120.7)
coalCons <- c(501.9, 1839.4, 117.7, 295.6, 90.9, 13.9)
ConsData <- cbind(country, oilCons, coalCons)
ConsData <- data.frame(ConsData)
ConsData$oilCons <- as.numeric(oilCons)
ConsData$coalCons <- as.numeric(coalCons)
```

Here are a few remarks about the above code sequence. First, the function c(), creates a vector of data, either character (in quotation marks), or numeric. Then, the function cbind(), brings together several vectors and forms a matrix with the vectors as columns. (Function rbind(), not shown, creates a matrix of row vectors.) The function data.frame() transforms the matrix into a data frame having the same name. A data frame is sometimes easier to use than a matrix. The symbol <-, as you may have already guessed, gives a name to the object at the right-hand side of the symbol. When creating the data frame, all data has been converted by R to character, following the type of the first column; therefore, I needed to convert the last two columns back into numerical type, using the function as.numeric.

Data sets in R are often organized as data frames, with "variables" in columns and "observations" in rows. Each variable has its name at the top of its column; rows can be given names as well, but often it is not necessary. A variable in a data frame can be separately accessed by the name of the data frame followed immediately by $ and the name of the variable, as in the following code example, which shows how to calculate the mean oil consumption in the ConsData data frame. The code also shows how to display a result just by introducing its name in a command line. Attributing a name to an object allows us to use the object later just by its name.

```
avgOilCons <- mean(ConsData$oilCons)
avgOilCons
```

```
## [1] 319.3
```

## 1.3 Data Sources

This guide will use the data required in the textbook Black (2017). The data are stored in the R package `Black9edata` (Colonescu 2016), which needs to be installed in your version of R and then loaded every time you open a new session, as we have already discussed. A particular file, say the file required by Problem 12.13 can be loaded using the command `data(p12.13)`. The `Black9edata` package includes, besides the data, descriptions of the variables in the "Dataset" collection. Since the data files for "Cases" and "Problems" do not have descriptions, these files do not show in the package description page; therefore, to open one of these files you should know the name of the data file you want to open.

Once the `Black9edata` package is installed and loaded, one can get a list of all the data files available as the following code shows.

```
data(package="Black9edata")
```

For completeness, though, here is the list of all the data files in the Black9edata package (these files are also available at the textbook website in other formats).

*Data sets*:

Energy, Gas12yr, Agri, Food, Financial, Hospital, Labor, Manufacturer, and Stock

*Cases*:

CaseCh2, CaseCh3, CaseCh9, CaseCh11Q1, CaseCh11Q2, CaseCh11Q3, CaseCh12Cost, CaseCh12Sales, CaseCh13Q1, CaseCh13Q2, CaseCh14Q1, CaseCh14Q2, CaseCh15Q1, CaseCh15Q2, CaseCh16Price, CaseCh16Sex, CaseCh17Q1, and CaseCh17Q2

*Problems*:

p2.01, p2.03, p2.09, p2.10, p2.15, p2.17, p2.20, p2.21, p2.25, p2.28, p2.29, p2.30, p2.31, p2.32, p2.33, p2.34, p2.37, p2.39, p2.42, p2.43, p2.44, p2.45, p2.46

## 1.3. DATA SOURCES

p3.1, p3.10, p3.11, p3.12, p3.13, p3.14, p3.15, p3.16, p3.18, p3.19, p3.2, p3.20, p3.26, p3.3, p3.37, p3.38, p3.39, p3.4, p3.40, p3.41, p3.42, p3.43, p3.44, p3.5, p3.50, p3.52, p3.6, p3.7, p3.8, p3.9

p5.21

p8.10, p8.11, p8.13, p8.14, p8.17, p8.19, p8.20, p8.21, p8.22, p8.23, p8.36, p8.38, p8.39, p8.48, p8.49, p8.51, p8.53, p8.57, p8.61, p8.71, p8.72, p8.8, p8.9

p9.11, p9.15, p9.16, p9.17, p9.18, p9.21, p9.22, p9.34, p9.35, p9.36, p9.52, p9.57, p9.6, p9.63, p9.64

p10.13, p10.14, p10.16, p10.19, p10.20, p10.21, p10.22, p10.24, p10.25, p10.26, p10.27, p10.3, p10.4, p10.41, p10.42, p10.50, p10.55, p10.62, p10.63, p10.64, p10.65, p10.70, p10.71, p10.8

p11.11, p11.12, p11.13, p11.14, p11.28, p11.29, p11.32, p11.33, p11.40, p11.41, p11.42, p11.43, p11.45, p11.47, p11.5, p11.50, p11.53, p11.55, p11.56, p11.57, p11.58, p11.59, p11.6, p11.60, p11.61, p11.7, p11.8

p12.1, p12.10, p12.11, p12.12, p12.13, p12.14, p12.15, p12.16, p12.17, p12.18, p12.2, p12.20, p12.21, p12.22, p12.3, p12.31, p12.37, p12.4, p12.48, p12.49, p12.5, p12.50, p12.51, p12.52, p12.53, p12.54, p12.55, p12.56, p12.57, p12.58, p12.59, p12.6, p12.60, p12.61, p12.62, p12.63, p12.64, p12.65, p12.66, p12.7, p12.8, p12.9

p13.1, p13.11, p13.12, p13.2, p13.24, p13.25, p13.26, p13.27, p13.28, p13.29, p13.30, p13.31, p13.5, p13.6

p14.1, p14.11, p14.13, p14.14, p14.17, p14.18, p14.2, p14.27, p14.28, p14.29, p14.3, p14.30, p14.31, p14.32, p14.33, p14.34, p14.35, p14.37, p14.4, p14.5, p14.6, p14.7, p14.8

p15.1, p15.10, p15.11, p15.12, p15.13, p15.14, p15.15, p15.17, p15.19, p15.2, p15.20, p15.21, p15.22, p15.23, p15.24, p15.25, p15.26, p15.27, p15.28, p15.29, p15.3, p15.30, p15.31, p15.32, p15.35, p15.36, p15.37, p15.38, p15.39, p15.4, p15.42, p15.43, p15.44, p15.5, p15.6, p15.7, p15.8, p15.9

p16.1, p16.10, p16.11, p16.12, p16.13, p16.14, p16.15, p16.17, p16.18, p16.19, p16.2, p16.24, p16.25, p16.3

p17.1, p17.10, p17.11, p17.12, p17.13, p17.14, p17.15, p17.16, p17.17, p17.18, p17.19, p17.2, p17.20, p17.21, p17.22, p17.23, p17.24, p17.25, p17.26, p17.27, p17.28, p17.31, p17.32, p17.33, p17.34, p17.35, p17.36, p17.37, p17.38, p17.39, p17.40, p17.41, p17.42, p17.43, p17.44, p17.45, p17.46, p17.47, p17.48, p17.49, p17.5, p17.50, p17.51, p17.52, p17.53, p17.54, p17.55, p17.56, p17.57, p17.58, p17.59, p17.6, p17.60, p17.7, p17.8, p17.9

p18.16, p18.17, p18.18, p18.19, p18.20, p18.21, p18.22, p18.23, p18.4, p18.5, p18.8, and p18.9.

For your information, the website https://mran.microsoft.com/documents/data/#econ lists a number of data sources that are available online.

# Chapter 2

# Charts and Graphs

## 2.1 Frequency Distributions

The next code sequence creates the function frdis(), which calculates frequency distributions for a given data vector and a given division (breaks) of the data (dta) in classes (classes are given in the argument breaks of the function). Once the function is created as an object (you can spot it in the "Environment" window), you can use it to answer any problem that requires building a frequency distribution table like Table 2.3 in the textbook. You can name this table when you use the function like this: tabname <- frdis().

```
#-------------------------------------------------------------------
#           Function: Frequency Distribution of a Vector
#-------------------------------------------------------------------
frdis <- function(dta, breaks){ # Curly bracket begins function
  bins<-cut(dta, breaks,include.lowest=TRUE,right=FALSE,
            na.rm=TRUE) # Sorts values into classes
  freq <- table(bins) # Calculate frequencies
  rel.freq <- freq/length(dta) #Relative frequency
  cm.freq <- cumsum(freq) # Cumulative frequency
  nint=length(breaks)-1 # Number of intervals
  midp <- rep(0,nint) # Initial midpoint vector of zeros
  for(i in 1:nint){ # Loop to calculate class midpoints
    midp[i]=(breaks[i+1]+breaks[i])/2 #Midpoints
  } # Curly bracket ends the 'for' loop
  frdis.res <- data.frame(cbind(freq, # Makes results table
```

```
                    midp, rel.freq, cm.freq))
  return(frdis.res)
}#                        End of Function
#-----------------------------------------------------------------
```

The code elements that we have used so far are:

- `seq()` splits an interval in a given number of equal parts
- `fname <- function(arguments){body}` creates the new function named fname
- `cut()` splits the data in groups according to a number of classes previously give (in our case, calculated by the function `seq()`)
- `table()`, which actually calculates the frequencies (number of data values in each class)
- `cumsum()` returns a cumulative sum of a series (vector) of numbers
- `length()` gives the number of elements in a vector or data frame
- `rep(0,n)` creates a vector containing n zeros.
- `for(i in N){body}` executes the set of commands in "body" N times
- `cbind()` puts together several column vectors into a data frame (table).

A first example of using the function `frdis()` with a textbook dataset solves Problem 2.1 in Cjhapter 2. Here is the code for part (a) of the problem. You can display the resulting distribution table by simply typing the name of the table in your script.

```
library(Black9edata)
data(p2.01)
dta <- p2.01$X__1 #a vector of data values
breaks <- seq(0,100,by=20)
dis.p2.01<-frdis(dta, breaks) #Ditrib. table for p2.01
dis.p2.01 #displays the calculated distribution table

##            freq midp rel.freq cm.freq
## [0,20)        7   10     0.14       7
## [20,40)      15   30     0.30      22
## [40,60)      12   50     0.24      34
## [60,80)      12   70     0.24      46
## [80,100]      4   90     0.08      50
```

A second example uses this newly created function to re-calculate Table 2.3 in the textbook, for which we need to introduce the data in Table 2.1 manually. The next code fragment illustrates this example, with the results stored in the data frame `dis.unempl`.

## 2.2. QUANTITATIVE DATA GRAPHS

```
unempl60 <- c(2.3,2.8,3.6,2.4,2.9,3.0,4.6,4.4,3.4,4.6,6.9,6.0,7.0,7.1,
              5.9,5.5,4.7,3.9,3.6,4.1,4.8,4.7,5.9,6.4,6.3,5.6,5.4,7.1,
              7.1,8.0,8.4,7.5,7.5,7.6,11.0,12.0,11.3,10.6,9.7,8.8,7.8,
              7.5,8.1,10.3,11.2,11.4,10.4,9.5,9.6,9.1,8.3,7.6,6.8,7.2,
              7.7,7.6,7.2,6.8,6.3,6.0)
intervals <- seq(1,13,by=2)
dis.unempl<-frdis(unempl60,intervals)#Distrib. table unemployment
dis.unempl
```

```
##          freq midp   rel.freq cm.freq
## [1,3)      4    2  0.06666667       4
## [3,5)     12    4  0.20000000      16
## [5,7)     13    6  0.21666667      29
## [7,9)     19    8  0.31666667      48
## [9,11)     7   10  0.11666667      55
## [11,13]    5   12  0.08333333      60
```

## 2.2 Quantitative Data Graphs

The following code lines create a histogram of Canadian unemployment data. Figure 2.1 shows the histogram.

```
hist(unempl60, intervals, main="",
     xlab="Unemployment Rates for Canada")
```

Next, we draw a frequency polygon and a cumulative frequency "ogive," as in Figures 2.5 and 2.6 in the textbook. We use the results stored by the function frdis() in the data frame dis.unempl.

```
plot(dis.unempl$midp,dis.unempl$freq,type="l",
  xlab="Unemployment rates for Canada",ylab="Frequency")
plot(dis.unempl$midp,dis.unempl$cm.freq,type="l",
     xlab="Unemployment Rates for Canada",
     ylab="Cumulative Frequency")
```

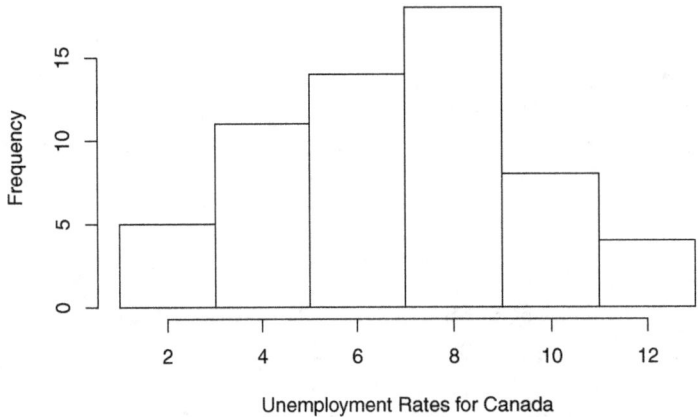

FIGURE 2.1 Histogram of Canadian Unemployment

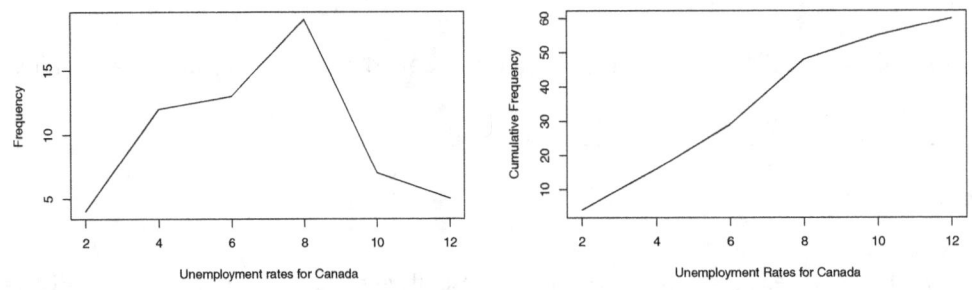

You can draw a **dot plot** using the function dotchart(data-vector).

```
dotchart(unempl60, xlab="Unemployment in Canada",font.lab=3)
```

## 2.3. QUALITATIVE DATA GRAPHS

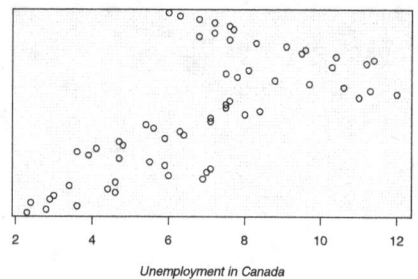
Unemployment in Canada

Constructing a stem-and leaf diagram for the employment data:

stem(unemp160)

```
## 
##    The decimal point is at the |
## 
##     2 | 3489
##     3 | 04669
##     4 | 1466778
##     5 | 45699
##     6 | 00334889
##     7 | 01112255566678
##     8 | 01348
##     9 | 1567
##    10 | 346
##    11 | 0234
##    12 | 0
```

## 2.3 Qualitative Data Graphs

The following example reproduces Table 2.6 in the textbook. The function pie() automatically calculates proportions and degrees. However, the second graph shows an alternative that shows the percentages along with the labels of different slices.

```
company<-c("Exxon Mobil","Valero Energy","Chevron",
           "ConocoPhillips","Marathon Oil")
```

```
capacity<-c(5589, 2777, 2540, 2514, 1714)
pie(capacity, company)
percentages<-round(capacity/sum(capacity)*100)
lab <- paste(company,percentages)
lab<-paste(lab,"%", sep="")
pie(capacity, labels=lab,col = rainbow(length(lab)))
```

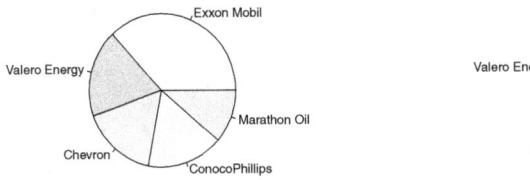

Let us construct a bar chart using data from Table 2.7; the R function for bar charts is barplot(). The example shows the same data, with both vertical and horizontal bars.

```
category<- c("Electronics", "Clothing and Accessories",
        "Dorm Furnishings","School Supplies","Misc.")
levels<-factor(category)
amount<-c(22.89,134.40,90.90,68.47,93.72)
op <- par(mar = c(5,11,4,2) + 0.1)# Makes more room to the left.
barplot(amount,names=category,horiz=TRUE,las=1,
        main="Back-to-College Spending ($)")
op <- par(mar = c(11,4,4,2) + 0.1)# Makes more room at the bottom.
barplot(amount,names=category,las=2,
        main="Back-to-College Spending ($)")
par(op) # Resets the figure margins parameters to default.
```

## 2.4. CHARTS AND GRAPHS FOR TWO VARIABLES

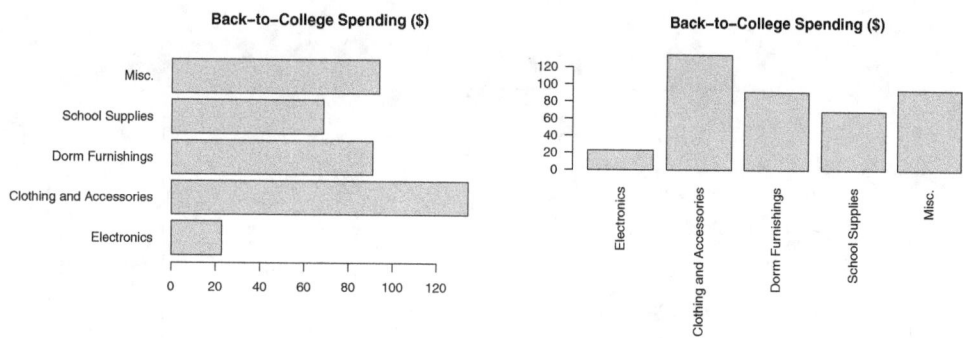

## 2.4 Charts and Graphs for Two Variables

**Cross tabulation** gives the frequency distribution counts of two variables simultaneously. The R function for cross tabulation is `table(x,y)`. Let us look at two variables in the Hospital database, where variable `region` can take integer values from 1 to 7 and the variable `ctrl` can take integer values from 1 to 4. The function `factor()` assigns meaningful labels to the categories in the variables, such that the generated contingency tables be easily to interpret.

```
data(Hospital)
head(Hospital)

## # A tibble: 6 x 12
##    hosp region  ctrl service  beds admiss census visits births totexp
##   <dbl>  <dbl> <dbl>   <dbl> <dbl>  <dbl>  <dbl>  <dbl>  <dbl>  <dbl>
## 1  1.00   1.00  2.00    1.00   210   7713    107  86982    312  56831
## 2  2.00   1.00  1.00    1.00   347  16065    198 149222   1077 127223
## 3  3.00   1.00  2.00    1.00   511  23028    356 222565   1027 157093
## 4  4.00   1.00  1.00    1.00   142   4338    100  36710    355  24462
## 5  5.00   7.00  1.00    1.00  40.0    905   9.00  13350    168  13730
## 6  6.00   4.00  2.00    1.00   220  15563    159  88721   3810  93257
## # ... with 2 more variables: payroll <dbl>, personnel <dbl>

region <- factor(Hospital$region, labels=c("S","NE","MW","SW",
                      "RM","CA","NW"))
owner <- factor(Hospital$ctrl,labels=c("GOV","NGO","FP","FED"))
table(region,owner)

##        owner
```

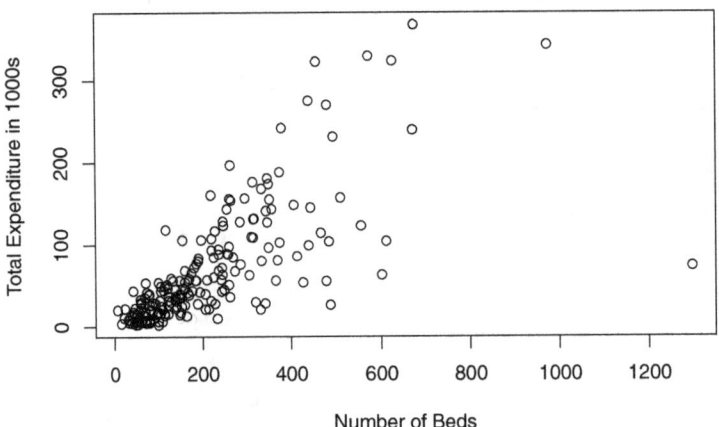

FIGURE 2.2 Scatterplot of Hospital Data

```
## region GOV NGO FP FED
##      S  17  17 18   4
##     NE   5  20  3   2
##     MW  16  25 11   8
##     SW   0   2  0   1
##     RM   7   9  3   1
##     CA   2   7  9   1
##     NW   4   6  1   1
```

A **scatter plot** shows points determined by pairs of values from two variables; one point in a scatter plot corresponds to one observation in the dataset. The next code and Figure 2.2 illustrate an example of a scatter plot.

```
library("Black9edata")
data("Hospital")
plot(Hospital$beds, Hospital$totexp/1000,
  xlab="Number of Beds", ylab="Total Expenditure in 1000s")
```

# Chapter 3

# Descriptive Statistics

Some of the examples in this chapter use data frome the `Black9edata` package, which, as always, needs to be loaded before being used.

`library(Black9edata)`

## 3.1 Measures of Central Tendency

In a dataset, the **mode** is the value that appears most often. If there are two values that appear by far more frequently than the others, the data is said to be *bimodal*. The following code, inspirad by (Williams 2011) calculates the mode for unimodal data.

```
#------------------------------------------------------------
#              Function:: Mode of a Set of Numbers
#------------------------------------------------------------
modf <- function(x){  # Variable x is the data vector.
unx <- unique(x)      # Eliminates the duplicates in x.
mtch <- match(x,unx)  # An index of x with order rank in unx.
tbl <- tabulate(mtch) # Counts frequency in mtch.
return(unx[which.max(tbl)]) # Identifies the most frequent unx.
}
#                    End of Function
#------------------------------------------------------------
```

Let us apply function `modf()` to the data in Table 3.1 in the textbook and to variables `region` and `Ownership (ctrl)` in the Hospital database.

```
# Table 3.1 data:
prices <- c(14.25,24,27,34.22,19,19,23,25,15.5,19,
            11,43.25,15,15,27,28,19,7,22,21)
modPrices <- modf(prices)
modPrices
```

```
## [1] 19
```

```
# Region in the Hospital database
modRegion <- modf(Hospital$region)
modRegion
```

```
## [1] 3
```

```
# Ownership in the Hospital database
modCtrl <- modf(Hospital$ctrl)
modCtrl
```

```
## [1] 2
```

In an ordered array, the **median** is the value of the middle element of the array (the element in the position $(n+1)/2$ of the ordered array); half of the numbers are less, and half greater than the median number. If the number of elements in the array is odd, then the median is the value in the middle; if the number of elements in the array is even, then the median is the arithmetic mean of the two numbers in the middle of the array. For instance, the median of the array $a = \{1, 5, 6\}$ is 5, and the median of the array $b = \{1, 5, 6, 7\}$ is 5.5. If there are missing values (NA) in the data, R can be instructed to remove the missing values before calculating the median using the argument na.rm=TRUE; otherwise, R returns NA as the result of calculating the median.

```
a <- c(1,5,6)
b <- c(1,5,6,7)
d <- c(1,5,6,as.numeric(NA))
median(a)
```

```
## [1] 5
```

```
median(b)
```

```
## [1] 5.5
```

## 3.1. MEASURES OF CENTRAL TENDENCY

```
median(d)

## [1] NA

median(d, na.rm=TRUE)

## [1] 5
```

The function as.numeric() used in the above code sequence converts the missing value symbol NA to the same data type as the other elements in the array, which, in this case, is numeric.

The **mean** is the arithmetic mean (average) of a group of numbers; it is equal to the sum of all numbers divided by the number of numbers in the group. The same remarks apply about missing values as for the median. The R function for calculating the mean is mean().

```
a <- seq(from=1, to=105 , by=3) #Vector={1,4,7 ...,105}
mean(a)

## [1] 52
```

A number in an ordered array of data is in the 72nd **percentile** if it is greater than 72% of the data in the array and less than 27% of the data. A percentile, like the median, may not be a value among those in the dataset.

Let us reproduce *Demonstration Problem 3.2*. The R function quantile() calculates percentiles and does not require the data to be previously ordered. The function requires, as arguments, the name of the data vector and a vector of percentiles (probabilities) that the user wants to be calculated. The argument type determines the method of calculating percentiles. Different methods give slightly different results.

```
dp3.2 <- c(14,12,19,23,5,13,28,17)
quantile(dp3.2, probs=c(.3, .5, .75), type=1)

## 30% 50% 75%
##  13  14  19
```

The first, the second, and the third **quartile** of an ordered array are the 25th, 50th, and 75th percentiles. The following code fragment demonstrates calculating quartiles for the *Demonstration Problem 3.3*. The R function summary() also gives the quartiles, but does not allow choosing the method. Therefore, the results may differ from using the quantile() function.

```
spending<-c(22195,19526,9538,7793,7707,4023,3916,3576,3571,
            3553,3247,2488,2433,2050,1137,699)
quantile(spending, probs=c(.25,.50,.75), type=2)
```

```
##    25%    50%    75%
## 2460.5 3573.5 7750.0
```

```
summary(spending)
```

```
##    Min. 1st Qu.  Median    Mean 3rd Qu.    Max.
##     699    2474    3574    6091    7728   22195
```

## 3.2 Measures of Variability: Ungrouped Data

The **range** is the difference between the highest and the lowest numbers in a dataset. The range() function in R returns the minimum and the maximum valueas in the dataset, and the diff() function returns the differences between subsequent elements of an array; if the array only has two elements, then diff() returns the difference between the two elements. The function round() instructs R to display a result with a given number of decimals.

```
# Example: the range of the variable "beds" in "Hospital"
rge <- range(Hospital$beds)
diff(rge) # This is the sample range.
```

```
## [1] 1290
```

```
# Another example, using randomly generated data:
set.seed(12345) # Sets the random number seed.
x <- 20*rnorm(100) # Generates 100 random numbers.
round(diff(range(x)),2) # The range, rounded at 2 decimals.
```

```
## [1] 97.15
```

The **interquartile range** is the range between the first and the third quartiles. Here is the interquartile range for the data at page 55 of the textbook.

## 3.2. MEASURES OF VARIABILITY: UNGROUPED DATA

```
exports <- c(312.4,240.2,123.7,66.8,53.8,49.4,44.5,43.1,
             42.4,40.9,34.8,31.3,30.2,26.7,22.2)
q1and3 <- quantile(exports, probs=c(.25,.75), type=2)
diff(q1and3) # Interquartile range
```

```
##   75%
## 35.5
```

The **mean absolute deviation** is the average of the differences, in absolute values, between each number in an array and the mean of the array; the **variance** is the sum of the same differences, but squared, divided by the number of values plus 1; the **standard deviation** is the square root of the variance. These three measures of variability are demonstrated here using the data in the *Demonstration Problem 3.6*. The mean absolute deviation is calculated by the function aad() (average absolute deviation), the variance by var(), and standard deviiation by sd(). The following example also calculates the **z-score** (a deviation from the mean measured in standard deviations), and the **coefficient of variation**, which is the ratio between the standard deviation and the mean, in percentage.

```
#-------------------------------------------------------
#            Function: Coefficient of Variation
#-------------------------------------------------------
coefv <- function(x){ # Variable x is a numerical vector.
return(sd(x)/mean(x)*100)
}
#                    End of Function
#-------------------------------------------------------
```

```
x <- c(55,100,125,140,60)
xbar <- mean(x)
library(lsr) # Loads the package containing aad().
aad(x); # mean absolute deviation
```

```
## [1] 30.8
```

```
var(x) # variance
```

```
## [1] 1442.5
```

```r
sd(x)   # standard deviation
```

```
## [1] 37.98026
```

```r
scale(x) # z-scores for all x
```

```
##              [,1]
## [1,] -1.0795082
## [2,]  0.1053179
## [3,]  0.7635546
## [4,]  1.1584966
## [5,] -0.9478609
## attr(,"scaled:center")
## [1] 96
## attr(,"scaled:scale")
## [1] 37.98026
```

```r
coefv(x) # coefficient of variation
```

```
## [1] 39.56277
```

Let us reproduce the examples on page 67 of the textbook using the newly created function coefv().

```r
prices <- c(57,68,64,71,62)
n <- length(prices)# the number of observations in the data
mean(prices)
```

```
## [1] 64.4
```

```r
sd(prices)
```

```
## [1] 5.412947
```

```r
coefv(prices)
```

```
## [1] 8.405198
```

The results are different from the ones in the textbook because the functions var(), sd(), and coefv() use the sample formulas (divide the sum of squared deviations by n-1), while the textbook uses the population formula (divides by n). The following code calculates the standard deviation using both formulas, showing that the population formula gives the same result as in the textbook.

## 3.3. CENTRAL TENDENCY AND VARIABILITY: GROUPED DATA

```r
sqrt(sum((prices-mean(prices))^2)/(n-1)) #this is s (sample)
```

```
## [1] 5.412947
```

```r
sqrt(sum((prices-mean(prices))^2)/n) #sigma (population)
```

```
## [1] 4.841487
```

## 3.3 Central Tendency and Variability: Grouped Data

```r
data("Hospital")

# Mean by region:
expMeans <- aggregate(Hospital$totexp, by=list(Hospital$region),
                  FUN="mean")
names(expMeans)<-c("region", "averages of total expenditure")
expMeans
```

```
##   region averages of total expenditure
## 1      1                      61650.82
## 2      2                      94887.33
## 3      3                      58472.42
## 4      4                      48288.67
## 5      5                      71945.00
## 6      6                      60434.63
## 7      7                      74043.83
```

```r
# Median by region:
expMedians<-aggregate(Hospital$totexp, by=list(Hospital$region),
                  FUN="median")
names(expMedians) <- c("region", "medians of total expenditure")
expMedians
```

```
##   region medians of total expenditure
## 1      1                      44491.0
## 2      2                      52214.0
## 3      3                      29822.0
## 4      4                      45458.0
```

```
## 5      5                              44505.5
## 6      6                              60080.0
## 7      7                              48884.5
```
```r
# Standard deviation by region:
expSD<-aggregate(Hospital$totexp, by=list(Hospital$region),
                 FUN="sd")
names(expSD)<-c("region","std. deviations of total expenditure")
expSD
```
```
##   region std. deviations of total expenditure
## 1      1                              62287.33
## 2      2                             100444.47
## 3      3                              66086.46
## 4      4                              43621.94
## 5      5                              76211.51
## 6      6                              41835.59
## 7      7                              63488.47
```
```r
# Mean by region and ownership:
expTwoFact<-aggregate(Hospital$totexp,
          by=list(Hospital$region,Hospital$ctrl),FUN="mean")
names(expTwoFact) <- c("region", "ownership",
                       "averages of total expenditure")
expTwoFact
```
```
##    region ownership averages of total expenditure
## 1       1         1                      76738.235
## 2       2         1                     157636.200
## 3       3         1                      37963.688
## 4       5         1                      80667.286
## 5       6         1                      60161.000
## 6       7         1                      21497.500
## 7       1         2                      68069.294
## 8       2         2                      97256.900
## 9       3         2                      88604.880
## 10      4         2                      49704.000
## 11      5         2                      58315.667
## 12      6         2                      81365.857
## 13      7         2                      91747.500
## 14      1         3                      33943.500
## 15      2         3                       8272.333
```

## 3.3. CENTRAL TENDENCY AND VARIABILITY: GROUPED DATA

```
## 16       3       3              22859.091
## 17       5       3             109149.667
## 18       6       3              48675.000
## 19       7       3              75810.000
## 20       1       4              94933.750
## 21       2       4              44242.000
## 22       3       4              54294.250
## 23       4       4              45458.000
## 24       5       4              21939.000
## 25       6       4              20300.000
## 26       7       4             176241.000
```

When the variable we want to use for grouping is continuous, we can use the function table() to create groups. For instance, we would like to see average expenditure by personnel in the database Hospital.

```
bins <- cut(Hospital$personnel,breaks=5)
means <- aggregate(Hospital$totexp, by=list(bins),
                FUN="mean")
names(means)<- c("personnel category", "average expenditure")
means
```

```
##        personnel category average expenditure
## 1              (46,857]            30238.63
## 2           (857,1.66e+03]          95454.78
## 3     (1.66e+03,2.47e+03]          143724.71
## 4     (2.47e+03,3.28e+03]          233475.14
## 5     (3.28e+03,4.09e+03]          312724.00
```

But how do we calculate the overall mean of a dataset when we only have access to groups, but not to the raw data? Let us re-create Table 3.7 using the function frdis that we constructed in chapter 2. (You may need to run the function again to load it into the Environment.)

```
unempl60 <- c(2.3,2.8,3.6,2.4,2.9,3.0,4.6,4.4,3.4,4.6,6.9,6.0,7.0,7.1,
              5.9,5.5,4.7,3.9,3.6,4.1,4.8,4.7,5.9,6.4,6.3,5.6,5.4,7.1,
              7.1,8.0,8.4,7.5,7.5,7.6,11.0,12.0,11.3,10.6,9.7,8.8,7.8,
              7.5,8.1,10.3,11.2,11.4,10.4,9.5,9.6,9.1,8.3,7.6,6.8,7.2,
              7.7,7.6,7.2,6.8,6.3,6.0)
intervals <- seq(1,13,by=2)
tb<-frdis(dta=unempl60,breaks=intervals)# distrib. table unemployment
```

```
tb
```

```
##          freq midp   rel.freq cm.freq
## [1,3)       4    2 0.06666667       4
## [3,5)      12    4 0.20000000      16
## [5,7)      13    6 0.21666667      29
## [7,9)      19    8 0.31666667      48
## [9,11)      7   10 0.11666667      55
## [11,13]     5   12 0.08333333      60
```

Now, let us calculate the mean of the dataset using the grouped data.

```
nint<-length(tb$freq)
N<- tb$cm.freq[nint]
mu <- sum(tb$freq*tb$midp)/N
round(mu,2) # the mean of grouped data
```

```
## [1] 6.93
```

The following code sequence is a function that calculates the mean of grouped data when the classes and frequencies are given.

```
#--------------------------------------------------------------------
#                Function: Mean of Grouped Data
#--------------------------------------------------------------------
meanGroup <- function(breaks, freqs){
  nint<-length(freqs)
  N<-sum(freqs)
  M<-rep(0,nint)
  for(i in 1:nint){
    M[i]<-(breaks[i]+breaks[i+1])/2 # midpoints
  }
  mean<-sum(M*freqs)/N
  return(mean)
}
#                     End of Function
#--------------------------------------------------------------------
```

Now, check if the function works well using the same employment data as before, assuming that we have already calculated the breaks (interval limits) and the frequencies.

## 3.3. CENTRAL TENDENCY AND VARIABILITY: GROUPED DATA

```
mu <- meanGroup(intervals, tb$freq)
round(mu,2)
```

```
## [1] 6.93
```

```
#------------------------------------------------------------
#            Function: Median of Grouped Data
#------------------------------------------------------------
medianGroup <- function(breaks, freqs){
 nint <- length(freqs)
 cm.freq <- cumsum(freqs)
 midfreq<-cm.freq[nint]/2
  for(i in 1:nint){
    if(midfreq > cm.freq[i] & midfreq <= cm.freq[i+1]){
               midint <-i+1}
  }
 L <- breaks[midint]
 cfp <-cm.freq[midint-1]
 fmed <- freqs[midint]
 N <- cm.freq[nint]
 W <- breaks[midint+1]-breaks[midint]
 median <- L+((N/2-cfp)/fmed)*W
 return(median)
}
#            End of Function
#------------------------------------------------------------
```

If we apply this newly created function to the data in Table 3.6 of the textbook, we obtain the results shown in Table 3.7.

```
median <- medianGroup(breaks=intervals,freqs=tb$freq)
median
```

```
## [1] 7.105263
```

The **mode** of grouped data is the midpoint of the class with the highest frequency. Here is a function that determines the mode of grouped data.

```
#-----------------------------------------------------------------
#              Function: Mode of Grouped Data
#-----------------------------------------------------------------
modeGroup <- function(breaks, freqs){
  nint <- length(freqs)
  classes <- breaks[1:nint]
  dfr <- data.frame(cbind(classes, freqs))
  modcls <- dfr$classes[which.max(dfr$freqs)]

  for(i in 1:nint+1){
    if(breaks[i]==modcls){
      mode <- breaks[i]+(breaks[i+1]-breaks[i])/2}
  }
  return(mode)
} #                    End of Function
# -----------------------------------------------------------------
```

Let us find the mode for the grouped unemployment data, whith the vector `intervals` containing the break points of the classes (see Table 3.6)

```
mode<-modeGroup(intervals,tb$freq)
mode
```

```
## [1] 8
```

The **population variance** of grouped data is given by the formula

$$\sigma^2 = \frac{\sum f_i(M_i - \mu)^2}{N}$$

, where

- $f_i$ = frequency in class $i$
- $M_i$ = midpoint of class $i$
- $N$ = sum of all frequencies (= number of observations)
- $\mu$ = grouped mean of the population

The same formula gives the **sample variance**, but $N$ should be replaced with $n-1$. Here is a function that calculates the population variance and standard deviation of grouped data.

## 3.3. CENTRAL TENDENCY AND VARIABILITY: GROUPED DATA

```
#---------------------------------------------------------------
#             Function: Population Variance of Grouped Data
#---------------------------------------------------------------
varGroup <- function(breaks, freqs){
  nint <- length(freqs)
  N<-sum(freqs)
  mu <- meanGroup(breaks,freqs)
  M <- rep(0,nint)
  for(i in 1:nint){
    M[i]<-(breaks[i]+breaks[i+1])/2
  }
  freqs*(M-mu)^2
  var <- sum(freqs*(M-mu)^2)/N
  return(var)
} #                                End of Function
#---------------------------------------------------------------
```

Let us apply the varGroup function on the employment data.

```
variance<-varGroup(intervals, tb$freq)
round(variance, 2)
```

## [1] 7.13

The standard deviation of the grouped data is just the square root of the variance, $\sigma = \sqrt{7.129}$, which is equal to 2.67.

For another exercise, let us apply these functions to the data in *Demonstration Problem 3.7*.

```
breaks<-seq(from=10, to=50, by=5)
frequences<-c(6,22,35,29,16,8,4,2)
meanGroup(breaks,frequences)     #Mean
```

## [1] 25.65574

```
medianGroup(breaks,frequences)   #Median
```

## [1] 24.71429

```
modeGroup(breaks,frequences)     #Mode
```

## [1] 22.5

```
varGroup(breaks,frequences)       #Variance
```

```
## [1] 56.63968
```

```
(stdev<-sqrt(varGroup(breaks,frequences)))  #Standard deviation
```

```
## [1] 7.525934
```

The last line of code shows how enclosing a command in brackets forces the display of the result. (Normally, a named object is not displayed.)

## 3.4 Measures of shape

A distribution is **skewed** when it lacks symmetry, that is, when one tail is thicker than the other. Skewness is zero for a symmetric distribution; it is negative if the distribution has a longer tail to the left (the distribution is skewed to the left), and it is positive if the tail is longer to the right. In absolute value, the larger is the number representing skewness, the more asymmetric is the distribution.

```
library(moments)
data(Hospital)
skewness(Hospital$beds)
```

```
## [1] 2.248751
```

```
hist(Hospital$beds,freq=FALSE,
     main="A Right-Skewed Distribution",
     xlab="Hospital Beds")
lines(density(Hospital$beds, adjust=2))
```

## 3.4. MEASURES OF SHAPE

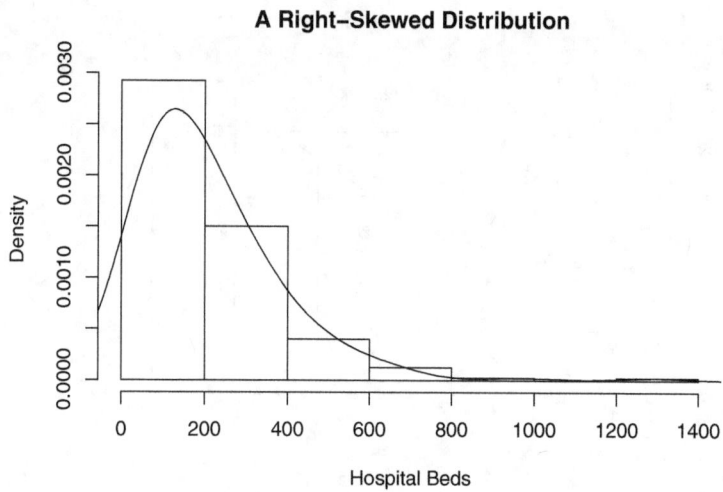

And here is an example of a left-skewed distribution:

```
example <- c(0,2,2,3,3,3,4,4,4,4,4,5,5,5,5,5,6,6,6,6,6,6,7)
skewness(example)
```

```
## [1] -0.7615818
```

```
hist(example, freq=FALSE,
     main="A Left-Skewed Distribution",
     xlab="Given Values")
lines(density(example), adjust=2)
```

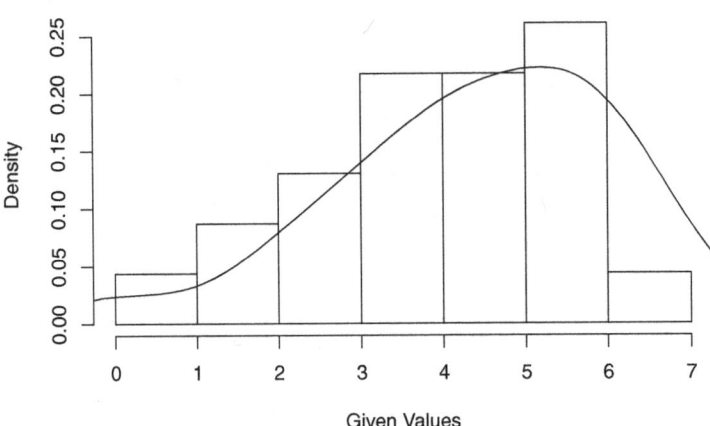

**A Left-Skewed Distribution**

**Kurtosis** is another shape parameter describing a distribution. If a distribution is tall and thin, it is called **leptokurtic**; if it is short and thick it is called **platykurtic**; if it is somehow in-between (looking "normal"), it is called **mesokurtic**.

A **boxplot** as the one presented in the next code sequence is another way of illustrating a distribution. It shows the second quartile (the median), the other quartiles, as well as the outliers. A longer whisker indicates skewness. Closely related to the boxplot, the **five-number** statistic displays, in order, the lower end of the lower whisker, the lower "hinge," (the first quartile) the median, the upper "hinge" (the third quartile) , and the higher end of the upper whisker.

```
data(Hospital)
boxplot(Hospital$beds)
```

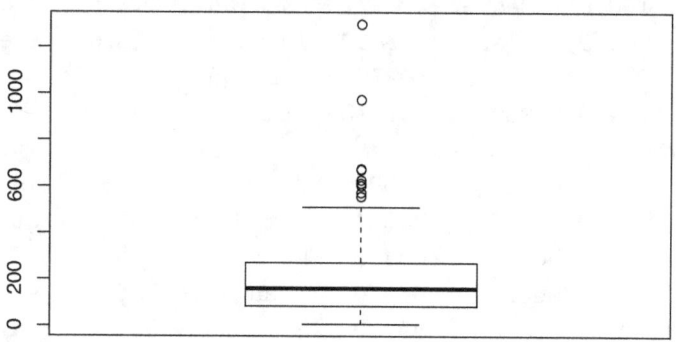

```
fivenum(Hospital$beds)
```

```
## [1]    7   84  160  271 1297
```

## 3.5  Descriptive Statistics in R

The function `summary()` applies to a variety of objects, among which unique variables and data frames.

```
summary(Hospital$visits) #For a variable
```

```
##    Min. 1st Qu.  Median    Mean 3rd Qu.    Max.
##       0   27316   65329   98225  123263  813369
```

```
summary(Hospital) #For a data frame
```

```
##       hosp            region          ctrl           service
##  Min.   :  1.00   Min.   :1.00   Min.   :1.00   Min.   :1.00
##  1st Qu.: 50.75   1st Qu.:1.00   1st Qu.:1.00   1st Qu.:1.00
##  Median :100.50   Median :3.00   Median :2.00   Median :1.00
##  Mean   :100.50   Mean   :3.03   Mean   :2.15   Mean   :1.16
##  3rd Qu.:150.25   3rd Qu.:5.00   3rd Qu.:3.00   3rd Qu.:1.00
##  Max.   :200.00   Max.   :7.00   Max.   :4.00   Max.   :2.00
##      beds             admiss          census          visits
```

```
## Min.   :   7.0   Min.   :  111   Min.   :   2.00   Min.   :     0
## 1st Qu.:  84.5   1st Qu.: 1615   1st Qu.:  47.75   1st Qu.: 27316
## Median : 160.0   Median : 4777   Median : 102.50   Median : 65329
## Mean   : 209.9   Mean   : 6832   Mean   : 144.09   Mean   : 98225
## 3rd Qu.: 270.0   3rd Qu.: 9766   3rd Qu.: 181.75   3rd Qu.:123263
## Max.   :1297.0   Max.   :37375   Max.   :1106.00   Max.   :813369
##      births           totexp           payroll          personnel
## Min.   :   0     Min.   :  2082   Min.   :  1053   Min.   :  50.0
## 1st Qu.:   0     1st Qu.: 20544   1st Qu.:  8693   1st Qu.: 314.0
## Median : 480     Median : 43365   Median : 20740   Median : 589.5
## Mean   : 874     Mean   : 67140   Mean   : 30501   Mean   : 861.5
## 3rd Qu.:1309     3rd Qu.: 89899   3rd Qu.: 40275   3rd Qu.:1095.2
## Max.   :5699     Max.   :367706   Max.   :188865   Max.   :4087.0
```

The following examples show alternative ways of finding descriptive statistics in R.

```
# The function `sapply()` applies a function to a list or vector.
# For descriptive statistics, the function could be mean, sd, var,
# min, max, median, range, and quantile.
sapply(list(Hospital$census), mean, na.rm=TRUE)
```

```
## [1] 144.095
```

```
# install.packages("Hmisc") #If not already installed
library(Hmisc)
# The numbers .05, .10, ... are percentiles.
describe(Hospital$census)
```

```
##    vars   n   mean     sd  median  trimmed   mad  min   max  range  skew
## X1    1 200 144.09 149.57  102.5   117.59  94.89    2  1106   1104  2.88
##    kurtosis    se
## X1    12.26 10.58
```

```
# install.packages("pastecs") # If not installed yet.
library(pastecs)
# Results: number of values, number of zeros, number of
# missing values, min, max, range, sum, median, mean, SE.mean,
```

## 3.5. DESCRIPTIVE STATISTICS IN R

```
# 95% confidence interval of the mean, var, std.dev, and coef.var
stat.desc(Hospital$census)
```

```
##        nbr.val      nbr.null        nbr.na           min           max
##     200.000000      0.000000      0.000000      2.000000   1106.000000
##          range           sum        median          mean       SE.mean
##    1104.000000  28819.000000    102.500000    144.095000     10.575925
## CI.mean.0.95           var       std.dev      coef.var
##      20.855264  22370.036156    149.566160      1.037969
```

The function describe() in package psich takes a data frame or a matrix for its first argument, which is the item to be described.

```
# install.packages("psich") # if not installed yet
library(psych)
# The list of results include name, item number, nvalid, mean, sd,
# median, mad, min, max, skew, kurtosis, and se.

describe(Hospital$totexp)
```

```
##    vars   n    mean       sd  median  trimmed      mad  min    max   range
## X1    1 200 67139.8 70386.44 43364.5 54206.22 42373.45 2082 367706  365624
##    skew kurtosis      se
## X1 1.98      4.3 4977.07
```

# Chapter 4

# Probability

The probability that an event E occurs is equal to the number of ways in which E can occur, $n_e$, divided by the total number of possible outcomes, $N$.

$$P(E) = \frac{n_e}{N}$$

Conditional probability is the probability that X happens given that Y has happened (the sample space of X is, in a conditional probability, restricted to the sample space of Y). We denote the probability of X given that Y has happened by

$$P(X|Y).$$

If X and Y are **independent**, then

$$P(X|Y) = P(X)$$

and

$$P(Y|X) = P(Y).$$

Joint probability is the probability that two events happen at the same time. We can present joint probabilities in a matrix or a data frame (joint probability table). For example, let us reproduce the *Demonstration Problem 4.1*.

```
jprobs<-c(.052,.2,.335,.058,.019,.084,.11,.142)
# Make a matrix with Sex on columns:
A<-matrix(jprobs, ncol=2, dimnames=list(
  c("Managerial","Professional","Technical","Clerical"),
  c("Male","Female")
```

```
))
Sex<-colSums(A) # vertical summation, marginal prob. of "Sex"
Position<-rowSums(A) # horiz. summation, marginal prob. of "Positions"
B<-cbind(A,Position) # Appends marginal prob. to joint table.
Sex<-c(Sex,sum(Sex))# Sum of marginal probabilities must be 1.
C<-rbind(B,Sex)# Appends marginal prob. of Sex to joint matrix.
C
```

```
##                  Male Female Position
## Managerial      0.052  0.019    0.071
## Professional    0.200  0.084    0.284
## Technical       0.335  0.110    0.445
## Clerical        0.058  0.142    0.200
## Sex             0.645  0.355    1.000
```

# Chapter 5

# Discrete Distributions

In R, probability distribution commands start with a letter that indicates the kind of operation needed, as follows. Suppose $X$ is a random variable and $x$ is a particular occurrence.

- p returns the probability $P(X \leq x)$ for a given $x$
- q gives the value of $x$ for a given probability $P(X \leq x)$
- d gives the density function for a given $x$
- r draws a random sample from a given distribution

To construct a specific command, you need to append the name of your distribution to one of these symbols, such as `pnorm()` for a normal distribution or `dchisq()` for a chi-squared distribution. Here is a list with the most often used distributions with their R symbols and arguments, as they appear in their `help` descriptions.

The normal distribution

- dnorm(x, mean = 0, sd = 1, log = FALSE)
- pnorm(q, mean = 0, sd = 1, lower.tail = TRUE, log.p = FALSE)
- qnorm(p, mean = 0, sd = 1, lower.tail = TRUE, log.p = FALSE)
- rnorm(n, mean = 0, sd = 1)

The *t*-distribution

- dt(x, df, ncp, log = FALSE)
- pt(q, df, ncp, lower.tail = TRUE, log.p = FALSE)
- qt(p, df, ncp, lower.tail = TRUE, log.p = FALSE)
- rt(n, df, ncp)

The chi-squared distribution

- dchisq(x, df, ncp = 0, log = FALSE)
- pchisq(q, df, ncp = 0, lower.tail = TRUE, log.p = FALSE)
- qchisq(p, df, ncp = 0, lower.tail = TRUE, log.p = FALSE)
- rchisq(n, df, ncp = 0)

The binomial distribution

Here, x and q are vectors of quantiles, size is the number of trials, prob is the probability of success in one trial, p is a vector of probabilities, and n is the number of observations.

- dbinom(x, size, prob, log = FALSE)
- pbinom(q, size, prob, lower.tail = TRUE, log.p = FALSE)
- qbinom(p, size, prob, lower.tail = TRUE, log.p = FALSE)
- rbinom(n, size, prob)

The Poisson distribution

- dpois(x, lambda, log = FALSE)
- ppois(q, lambda, lower.tail = TRUE, log.p = FALSE)
- qpois(p, lambda, lower.tail = TRUE, log.p = FALSE)
- rpois(n, lambda)

The hypergeometric distribution

Here, x is the number of successes in the sample, m is the number of successes in the population, n the number of failures in the population, and k the number of balls in the sample.

- dhyper(x, m, n, k, log = FALSE)
- phyper(q, m, n, k, lower.tail = TRUE, log.p = FALSE)
- qhyper(p, m, n, k, lower.tail = TRUE, log.p = FALSE)
- rhyper(nn, m, n, k)

The textbook symbols $N$, $n$, $A$, and $x$ are, respectively, replaced by m+n, k, m, and q or x.

The uniform distribution:

- dunif(x, min = 0, max = 1, log = FALSE)
- punif(q, min = 0, max = 1, lower.tail = TRUE, log.p = FALSE)
- qunif(p, min = 0, max = 1, lower.tail = TRUE, log.p = FALSE)
- runif(n, min = 0, max = 1)

The exponential distribution

Here, rate is a vector of rates

## 5.1 Statistics of a Discrete Distribution

- dexp(x, rate = 1, log = FALSE)
- pexp(q, rate = 1, lower.tail = TRUE, log.p = FALSE)
- qexp(p, rate = 1, lower.tail = TRUE, log.p = FALSE)
- rexp(n, rate = 1)

## 5.1 Statistics of a Discrete Distribution

```
x <- 0:5
px <- c(.37, .31, .18, .09, .04, .01)
(mu <- sum(x*px)) # mean, or expected value
```

```
## [1] 1.15
```

```
(variance <- sum((x-mu)^2*px)) # variance
```

```
## [1] 1.4075
```

```
(stdev <- sqrt(variance))
```

```
## [1] 1.186381
```

## 5.2 Binomial Distribution

The distribution of the number of successes in $n$ trials with only two possible outcomes is **binomial**. Such a distribution assumes that a success happens with probability $p$, that each trial is independent of the others, and that the probabilities of success and failure are constant. The binomial formula is

$$P(x) = \binom{n}{x} p^x (1-p)^{n-x}$$

where

- $n$ is the sample size
- $x$ is gthe number of successes desired
- $p$ is the probability of a success in a draw

The mean and standard deviation of a binomial distribution are

$$\mu = np$$

$$\sigma = \sqrt{npq}$$

Let us use the binomial distribution to reproduce *Demonstration Problem 5.2*, which asks what is the probability that exactly 19 out of 25 customers are satisfied.

```
p<-0.65; size<-25; x<-19
(prob <- dbinom(x,size,p))
```

```
## [1] 0.090778
```

The *Demonstration Problem 5.3* requires the probability that a number of 18 or more (e.g., strictly greater than 17) of clients leave because they feel unappreciated, unimportant, or taken for granted. The function pbinom() is the one to use in this case, with the option lower.tail=FALSE.

```
p<-.68; size<-20; q<-17
pbinom(q,size,p,lower.tail=FALSE)
```

```
## [1] 0.0234551
```

If, for some reason, we want to create a distribution table like Table 5.6 in the textbook, we need to create, first, a vector $x$ of numbers from 1 to 23. The following code sequence shows how to create such a table.

```
#Table 5.6
x<-1:23
round(dbinom(x,23,.64),6)
```

```
##  [1] 0.000000 0.000000 0.000001 0.000006 0.000037 0.000199 0.000858
##  [8] 0.003051 0.009040 0.022500 0.047273 0.084041 0.126420 0.160533
## [15] 0.171236 0.152209 0.111421 0.066027 0.030890 0.010983 0.002789
## [22] 0.000451 0.000035
```

```
#Table 5.8
x<-6:20; size<-20;p<-.14
(probs<-round(dbinom(x,size,p),4));sum(probs)
```

```
##  [1] 0.0353 0.0115 0.0030 0.0007 0.0001 0.0000 0.0000 0.0000 0.0000 0.0000
## [11] 0.0000 0.0000 0.0000 0.0000 0.0000
```

```
## [1] 0.0506
```

## 5.3. POISSON DISTRIBUTION

```
#The last command, sum(probs) calculates P(X>5).
```

The same final result as the one in Table 5.8 can be obtained using the argument lower.tail=FALSE in the function pbinom(), as follows:

```
x<-5; size<-20;p<-.14
(probs<-round(pbinom(x,size,p,lower.tail=FALSE ),4))
```

```
## [1] 0.0507
```

Here is a code fragment that reproduces the first part of Figure 5.2.

```
n<-8; p<-.2
x <- dbinom(0:n,size=n,prob=p)
barplot(x,names.arg=0:n)
```

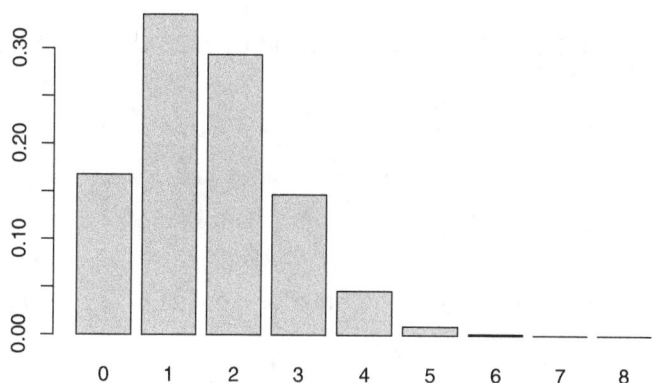

## 5.3 Poisson Distribution

The Poisson distribution gives the probabilities that rare events happen over a given period, such as the arrivals of customers in an hour. The foormula for the Poisson distribution is

$$P(x) = \frac{\lambda^x e^{-\lambda}}{x!}$$

where $x = 0, 1, 2, 3, ...,$ and $\lambda$ = long-run average of occurrences. The mean and the standard deviation of the Poisson distribution are

$$\mu = \lambda$$

$$\sigma = \sqrt{\lambda}$$

Let us reproduce the results in *Demonstration Problem 5.6*, which requires the probability that more than four customers arrive in a given minute if the long-run average is $\lambda = 2.3$ customers per minute.

```
l<-2.3; x<-4
(probs<- round(dpois(1:12,lambda=l),4))
```

```
## [1] 0.2306 0.2652 0.2033 0.1169 0.0538 0.0206 0.0068 0.0019 0.0005 0.0001
## [11] 0.0000 0.0000
```

```
(p4 <- sum(probs[(x+1):12]))
```

```
## [1] 0.0837
```

You obtain the same result if you use the function ppois(), as follows:

```
l<-2.3; x<-4
ppois(x,lambda=l,lower.tail=FALSE)
```

```
## [1] 0.08375072
```

Here is a graph of a Poisson distribution with $\lambda = 1.6$ (reproducing Figure 5.3 in the textbook).

```
par(mfrow=c(1,2))#Allows two graphs side by side
barplot(dpois(x=0:8,lambda=1.6), names.arg=0:8)
barplot(dpois(x=0:15,lambda=6.5),names.arg=0:15)
```

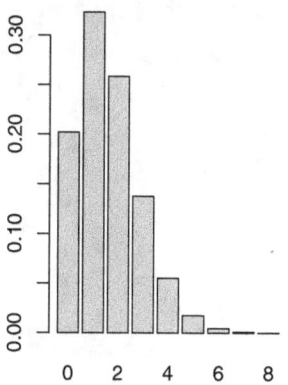 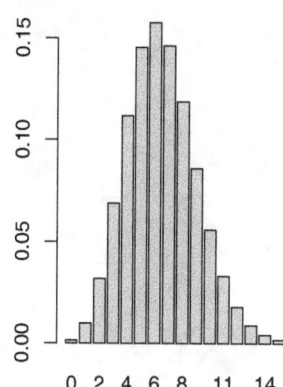

## 5.4 Hypergeometric Distribution

Like the binomial distribution, the hypergeometric distribution only allows for two possible outcomes, success or failure, but it requires that the trials are without replacement.

Let us reproduce the result in *Demonstration Problem 5.8*. Since we want the number of successes in the sample to be greater than or equal to 1, we need to set $q = 0$ when using phyper() with lower.tail=FALSE.

```
phyper(q=0, m=12, n=(18-12), k=3, lower.tail=FALSE)
```

```
## [1] 0.9754902
```

# Chapter 6

# Continuous Distributions

The function density() estimates the continuous distribution of a given univariate data set. Here is a simplified description of its use. density(x,adjust=1,na.rm = FALSE), where x is the data vector we wish to describe, and na.rm instructs R whether to remove the missing values (NA).

To construct an example, let us use the function rep(x,n), which produces a vector of length n of x identical numbers; function c(x,y,...) concatenates (links together, one after another) the vectors in its argument list, such as x and y. Figure 6.1 shows the result.

```
x<-c(rep(1,2),rep(3,4),rep(4,5),rep(5,2),rep(6,3),rep(7,2))
y<-density(x)
plot(y, ylim=c(0,.3), main=" ",
     xlab=" ")
hist(x,add=TRUE, freq=FALSE)
```

## 6.1 Uniform Distribution

A random variable is uniformly distributed when it can take any value, with equal probability, between the minimum $a$ and the maximum $b$. The distribution curve is a horizontal segment stretching from $a$ to $b$ at the height $1/(b-a)$, such that the area under the segment is, like the area under any probability density function, equal to 1.

To plot a uniform distribution, we first create an ordered vector x of numbers between $a$ and $b$, using, for example, the function seq(). For convenience, let us create a

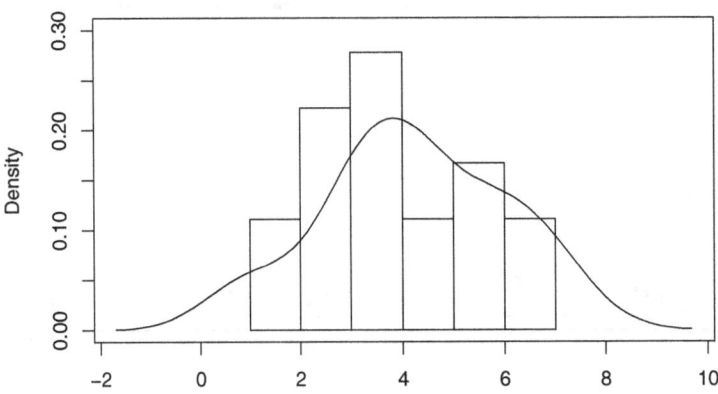

FIGURE 6.1 Histogrm of x

function to draw a uniform distribution between points $a$ and $b$; let us call this function `unifPlot(a,b)`.

```
#-----------------------------------------------------------------
#               Function: Plotting a Uniform Distribution
#-----------------------------------------------------------------
unifPlot<- function(a,b){
step<- (b-a)/100000
xmin<- a-0.1*(b-a)
xmax<-b+0.1*(b-a)
x=seq(xmin,xmax,by=step)
plot(x,dunif(x, min=a, max=b),
    xlab=expression(italic(x)),
    ylab="Density",
    type="l")
} #                                End of Function
#-----------------------------------------------------------------
```

While it is instructive to create one's own functions, it is also useful to know that the base R function `curve(expr,c,d)`, together with the function `dunif(x,a,b)` can easily draw a uniform distribution. Argument c is a number slightly less than a, and d is a number slightly greater than b; a and b are the limits of the desired uniform

## 6.1. UNIFORM DISTRIBUTION

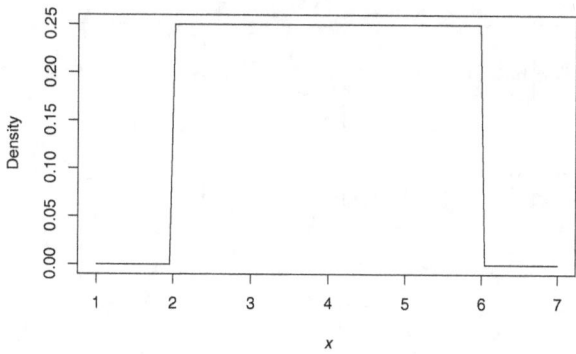

FIGURE 6.2 An Example of Uniform Distribution

distribution. Here is an example of using curve() with dunif() to plot a uniform distribution (see Figure 6.2).

```
curve(dunif(x,2,6),1,7,
      xlab=expression(italic(x)),
      ylab="Density")
```

Now, let us apply our newly created function unifPlot() to plot a uniform density function between 0 and 1, and another between 41 and 47. In the following code fragment, the function par allows drawing two graphs next to each other. Figure 6.3 shows the result.

```
a<-0
b<-1
par(mfrow=c(1,2))# To draw two graphs next to each other.
unifPlot(a,b)
a<-41
b<-47
unifPlot(a,b)
```

Researchers often use a distribution function to construct a sample of data drawn from that distribution. The following example shows how to draw a few samples of different sizes from a uniform distribution. The results suggest that, by increasing the sample size, the sample distribution approaches the theoretical one.

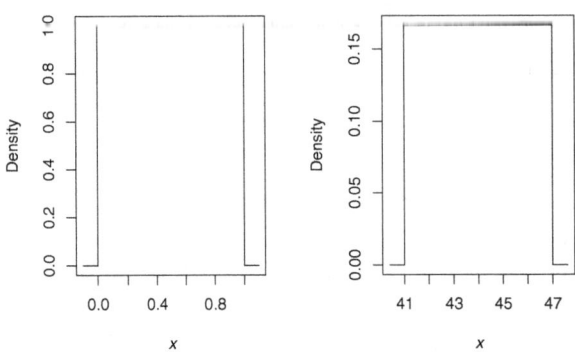

FIGURE 6.3 Two uniform distributions

```
set.seed=12345
x1<-runif(100);x2<-runif(1000);x3<-runif(100000);x4=runif(1000000)
par(mfrow=c(2,2))# Draws the graphs grouped in a 2 by 2 matrix
hist(x1,main="", xlab=expression(italic("x"[1])))
hist(x2,main="", xlab=expression(italic("x"[2])));
hist(x3,main="", xlab=expression(italic("x"[3])));
hist(x4,main="", xlab=expression(italic("x"[4])))
```

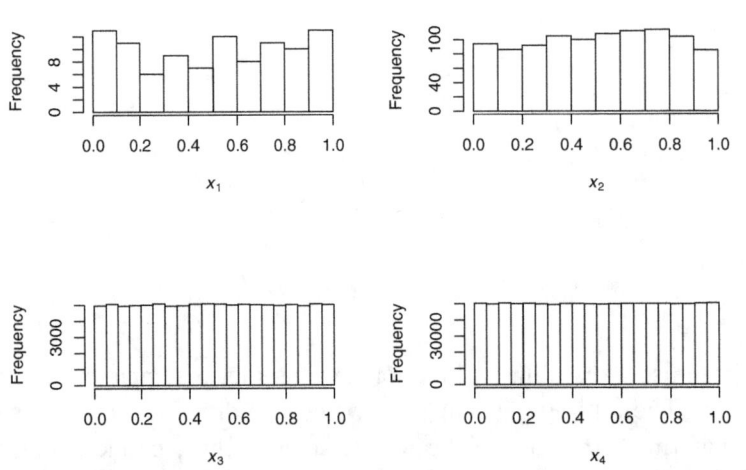

*Demonstration Problem 6.1* concerns a uniform distribution with parameters 27 and

## 6.2. NORMAL DISTRIBUTION

39. The problem requires the probability that the random variable is between 30 and 35. Here is the solution.

```
a<-27
b<-39
punif(35,27,39)-punif(30,27,39)
```

## [1] 0.4166667

To find the value of the variable (the quantile) when the probability is given, we can use the function qunif(). For instance, in the context of *Demonstration Problem 6.1*, if we are asked in how many seconds the task can be completed with a probability of 41.66667%, we can answer as follows:

```
a<-27
b<-39
p<-0.4166667
qunif(p,a,b)
```

## [1] 32

One could have expected this result, since the previous calculation showed that the probability of completing the task between 30 and 35 seconds was 0.4166667. But, with uniform distribution, the probability only depends on the *difference* in quantiles, not on their magnitude; thus, since $(35 - 30) = (32 - 27)$, the two probabilities must be equal.

## 6.2 Normal Distribution

As I have mentioned before, the R functions for the normal distribution are the following, where $x$ and $q$ are quantiles, $p$ is probability, and $n$ is the desired number of observations in a constructed sample:

- dnorm(x, mean = 0, sd = 1, log = FALSE)
- pnorm(q, mean = 0, sd = 1, lower.tail = TRUE, log.p = FALSE)
- qnorm(p, mean = 0, sd = 1, lower.tail = TRUE, log.p = FALSE)
- rnorm(n, mean = 0, sd = 1)

How to plot a normal distribution of given parameters? Let us first construct our own function, then see how the R function curve() can be used for the same purpose. First, we need to construct a unidimensional grid, $x$, then plot the points defined by all pairs (x, dnorm(x)). The argument ... indicates that more parameters, such as main = can be passed to the plot function

```
#-----------------------------------------------------------
#              Function: Plotting a Normal Distribution
#-----------------------------------------------------------
normPlot <- function(mu, sd, ...){
x<-seq(mu-3.5*sd,mu+3.5*sd,7*sd/100)
plot(x, dnorm(x,mu,sd), type="l",
     xlab=expression(italic("x")),
     ylab="Density", ...)
}
#                         End of Function
#-----------------------------------------------------------

par(mfrow=c(1,2))
normPlot(0,1,main="N(0,1)")
normPlot(44,9,main="N(44,9)")
```

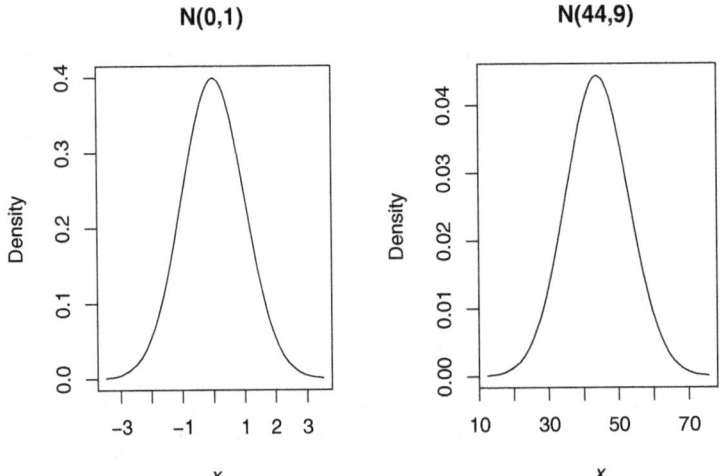

However, one can use the R functions curve() and dnorm() to plot a normal distribution, as follows (see Figure 6.4):

```
par(mfrow=c(1,2))
curve(dnorm(x,0,1),xlim=c(-3,3),xlab=expression(italic("x")))
curve(dnorm(x,44,9),xlim=c(15,70),xlab=expression(italic("x")))
```

## 6.2. NORMAL DISTRIBUTION

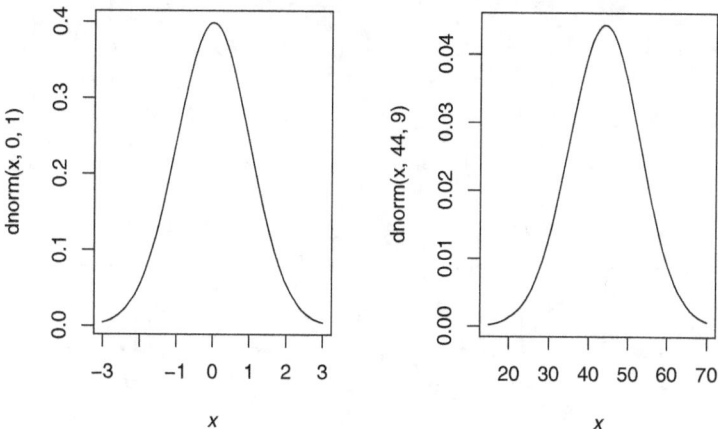

FIGURE 6.4 Using the Function 'curve' to Plot a Normal Distribution

If you need to find probabilities from the normal distribution, use the function pnorm(). Let us solve the *Demonstration Problem 6.3*, which requires the probability

$$P(3.6 < x < 5 \mid \mu = 4.43, \sigma = 1.32)$$

```
x1=3.6
x2=5
mu=4.43
sigma=1.32
(prob<-pnorm(x2,mu,sigma)-pnorm(x1,mu,sigma))
```

```
## [1] 0.4023192
```

Drawing a sample of $n$ observations from a normal distribution of mean mu and standard deviation sd requires the function rnorm(n,mu,sd). The following example constructs the histograms and the theoretical distributions for four samples of sizes 50, 100, 1000, and 10,000. You may disregard, for now, the complicated structure of the main argument in the function normPlot, which serves only at formatting the titles of the graphs. Figure 6.5 illustrates the four cases.

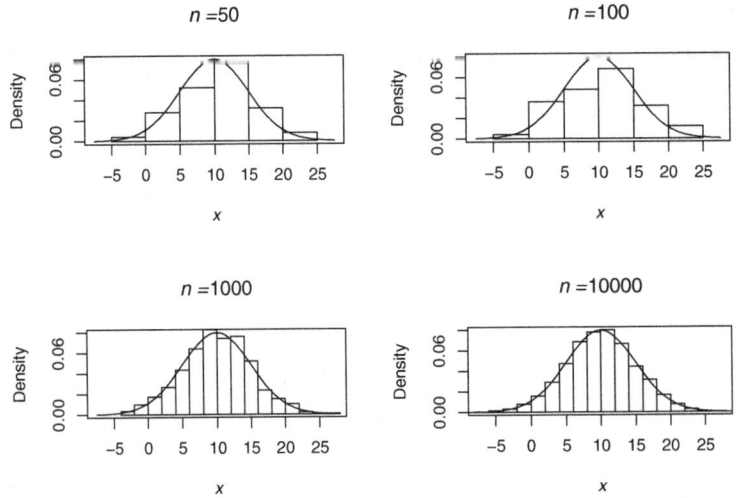

FIGURE 6.5 Histograms of Various Sample Sizes

```
par(mfrow=c(2,2)) # Creates a 2 x 2 matrix of graphs
set.seed(12345)
normPlot(10,5, main=expression(paste(italic("n ="),50)))
hist(rnorm(50,10,5),freq=FALSE,add=TRUE)
normPlot(10,5, main=expression(paste(italic("n ="),100)))
hist(rnorm(100,10,5),freq=FALSE,add=TRUE,xlab="Sample = 100")
normPlot(10,5, main=expression(paste(italic("n ="),1000)))
hist(rnorm(1000,10,5),freq=FALSE,add=TRUE)
normPlot(10,5, main=expression(paste(italic("n ="),10000)))
hist(rnorm(10000,10,5),freq=FALSE,add=TRUE)
```

## 6.3 Exponential Distribution

The exponential distribution describes the time between random occurrences; its probability density function is

$$f(x) = \lambda e^{-\lambda x}$$

Let us build a function to plot the exponential distribution.

## 6.3. EXPONENTIAL DISTRIBUTION

```
#-----------------------------------------------------------
#          Function: Plotting an Exponential Distribution
#-----------------------------------------------------------
expFun<-function(lambda,xmax, ...){
  x<-seq(0,xmax,0.1)
  plot(x, dexp(x,lambda),
       type="l", ...)
}#                                End of Function
#-----------------------------------------------------------
```

In the following code, where you may wish to disregard the complicated structures of the main, ylab, and xlab arguments, two examples of an exponential function are constructed. The resulting graphs are displayed in Figure 6.6.

```
par(mfrow=c(1,2))

lambda<-2.0
expFun(lambda,6, main=expression(paste(lambda, " = 2.0")),
       ylab=expression(paste("dexp(",italic(x),", ",lambda,")")),
       xlab=expression(paste(italic(x))))

lambda<-1.0
expFun(lambda,7, main=expression(paste(lambda, " = 1.0")),
       ylab=expression(paste("dexp(",italic(x),", ",lambda,")")),
       xlab=expression(paste(italic(x))))
```

The following example reproduces the results in Table 6.6 in the textbook, which uses an exponential distribution with $\lambda = 1.38$ defects per 20 minutes and requires the probability that less than 15 minutes pass before the next defect. The quantile ($q$) is equal to the ratio between the required interval (15) and the rate interval (20).

```
pexp(15/20,1.38,lower.tail=TRUE)
```

```
## [1] 0.6447736
```

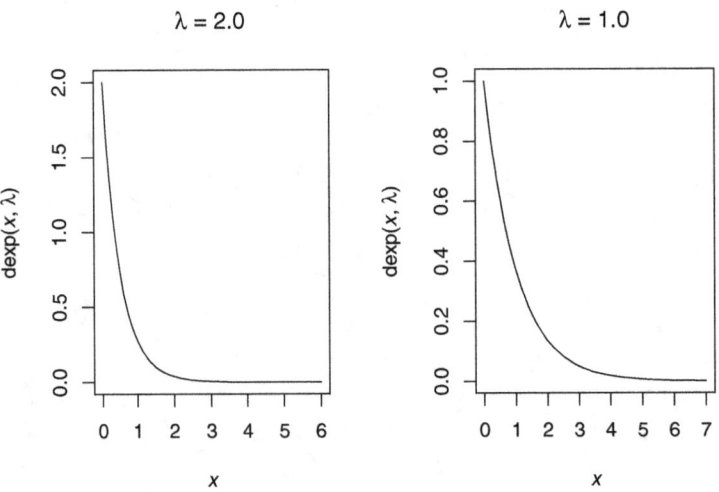

FIGURE 6.6 Two Examples of an Exponential Distribution

# Chapter 7

# Sampling and Sampling Distributions

## 7.1 Constructing a Random Sample

Suppose you are given a list of character values, such as the names of some companies, and you wish to select a random sample of 10. The following code constructs a simple function, based on the R function `sample()`, to extract a random sample of a given size from a vector (set) of numerical or character elements. The function requires two arguments: the initial vector x (the "population"), and the desired size of the sample, n. This newly created function samples without replacement. For more complex sampling tasks, such as sampling with replacement, you can use the R function `sample()`, but be careful because it may give unexpected results in some cases.

```
# #------------------------------------------------------------
#              Function: Random Sample from a Vector
#------------------------------------------------------------
randSampleVector <- function(x,size){
  N<-length(x)
  newSample<-x[sample(1:N,size)]
return(newSample)
} #                       End of Function
#------------------------------------------------------------
```

Here is an example of using our new function `randSampleVector()` to construct a sample of size 10 out of an ad-hoc created vector called population. I will use the function paste() to construct an array of character values.

```
n<-10
population <-paste("x",1:25,sep="")
set.seed(12345)# Set seed every time, if you want the same sample
rs10a<-randSampleVector(population,n)
rs10b<-sample(population,10)
population
```

```
##  [1] "x1"  "x2"  "x3"  "x4"  "x5"  "x6"  "x7"  "x8"  "x9"  "x10" "x11"
## [12] "x12" "x13" "x14" "x15" "x16" "x17" "x18" "x19" "x20" "x21" "x22"
## [23] "x23" "x24" "x25"
```

```
rs10a # A sample of 10:
```

```
##  [1] "x19" "x22" "x18" "x20" "x10" "x4"  "x7"  "x21" "x13" "x16"
```

```
rs10b # Another sample:
```

```
##  [1] "x1"  "x4"  "x17" "x25" "x9"  "x10" "x8"  "x19" "x24" "x16"
```

Le us examine a few more examples of using the function randSampleVector().

```
randSampleVector(1:30,5)
```

```
## [1] 14 10 28 20 17
```

```
randSampleVector(c(2,5,4,6,7,8,5,1,2,3,1,4,5),5)
```

```
## [1] 8 2 5 4 7
```

```
randSampleVector(c("Gigi","Gina","Gelu","Gica"),2)
```

```
## [1] "Gica" "Gigi"
```

For completeness, the next code sequence constructs a function that selects a random sample out of a data frame.

```
#-----------------------------------------------------
#              Function: Random Sample from a Data Frame
#-----------------------------------------------------
randSampleDf<-function(x,n){ # x is a dataframe.
  N<-nrow(x)
```

## 7.1. CONSTRUCTING A RANDOM SAMPLE

```
    smpl <- x[sample(1:N,n,replace=FALSE),]
    return(smpl)
} #                                End of Function
#-------------------------------------------------------------
```

Here is an example of a random sample from a dataframe, where the dataframe is made of a sequence of 100 numbers from 1 to 500 and 100 random numbers between 1 and 1000.

```
set.seed(12345)
a<-seq(1,500,length.out=100)
b<-randSampleVector(1:1000,100)
df<-data.frame(cbind(a,b))
smpl<-randSampleDf(df,10)
```

A **stratified random sample** is a random sample drawn from various categories in a population. Take the Hospital database, for example. If we wish to draw a subsample from the database, we would like it to be representative, with some observations coming from each region. The following code shows how to build a stratified random sample, whith the strata being the regions. (This part builds on a comment by Thomas at StackOverflow, May 5, 2014.)

```
set.seed(12345)
data("Hospital")
splt<-split(Hospital,Hospital$region)
sampls<-lapply(splt,
    function(x) x[sample(1:nrow(x),
    size=as.integer(0.5*nrow(x)), #half of obs from each stratum
    replace=FALSE),])
newHospital<-do.call(rbind,sampls)
```

A slightly different variation of the same code constructs a random sample using two stratification variables, as follows:

```
set.seed(12345)
data("Hospital")
splt<-split(Hospital,list(Hospital$region,Hospital$ctrl))
sampls<-lapply(splt,
```

```
  function(x) x[sample(1:nrow(x),
  size=as.integer(0.5*nrow(x)), #half of obs from each stratum
  replace=FALSE),])
newHospital<-do.call(rbind,sampls)
```

For a more user-friendly way of making a stratified random sample, one can build a function that wraps the previous commands in a compact, but, of course, less flexible function, as follows:

```
#--------------------------------------------------------------
#              Function: Stratified Random Sample
#--------------------------------------------------------------
stratSample<-function(dataframe,stratList,percent){
  splt<-split(dataframe,stratList)
sampls<-lapply(splt,
  function(x) x[sample(1:nrow(x),
  size=as.integer(percent*nrow(x)),
  replace=FALSE),])
newData<-do.call(rbind,sampls)
return(newData)
} #                                    End of Function
#--------------------------------------------------------------
```

Let us apply the newly created function to reproduce the sample from the file Hospital with percent=0.5.

```
set.seed(12345)
dataframe<-Hospital
stratList<-list(Hospital$region,Hospital$ctrl)
percent<-0.5
newHosp<- stratSample(dataframe,stratList,percent)
```

A **systematic sample** of size $n$ from a population of size $N$ includes every $k$-th element in the population frame, starting with a randomly chosen element from among the first $N - nk$ elements in the frame; $k$ is the integer part of the ratio $N/n$.

```
#--------------------------------------------------------------
#              Function: Systematic Sample
#--------------------------------------------------------------
systSample<-function(dataframe,n){
```

## 7.1. CONSTRUCTING A RANDOM SAMPLE

```
N<-nrow(dataframe)
k<-as.integer(N/n)
n1 <- N-n*k
startPoint<-sample(1:n1,1)
smplIndex<-seq(from=startPoint,to=startPoint+k*(n-1),by=k)
newData<-dataframe[smplIndex,]
return(newData)
} #                              End of Function
#------------------------------------------------------------------
```

To see how the new function works, let us apply it to the dataset Hospital to create a systematic sample of $n = 140$ observations.

```
set.seed(12345)
newHosp<-systSample(Hospital,88)
head(newHosp[1:5,1:9]) # Shows 5 rows and 9 columns.
```

```
## # A tibble: 5 x 9
##     hosp region  ctrl service  beds admiss census visits births
##    <dbl>  <dbl> <dbl>   <dbl> <dbl>  <dbl>  <dbl>  <dbl>  <dbl>
## 1   18.0   6.00  2.00    1.00   444  18258    219 170223   2450
## 2   20.0   6.00  3.00    1.00   247   5449    124  44425      0
## 3   22.0   6.00  2.00    1.00   236  11301    142  90178   2275
## 4   24.0   6.00  1.00    1.00   228  10444    140  95649   1313
## 5   26.0   6.00  2.00    1.00   273   9249    154  51102   1689
```

**Cluster (area) sampling** randomly selects a number of *clusters* and picks all, or a random sample from each of the selected clusters. Each cluster is assumed to have about the same composition as the population. Let us construct a simple function that selects a random sample of clusters and picks all observations in each cluster. In this function, x is the initial dataframe, clusterVariable is the variable in x that we use for clustering, and n is how many clusters we want.

```
#------------------------------------------------------------------
#                    Function: Cluster Sample
#------------------------------------------------------------------
clusterSample<-function(x,clusterVariable,n){
clusters<-as.numeric(randSampleVector(1:max(clusterVariable),n))
newData<-x[clusterVariable %in% clusters,]
return(newData)
```

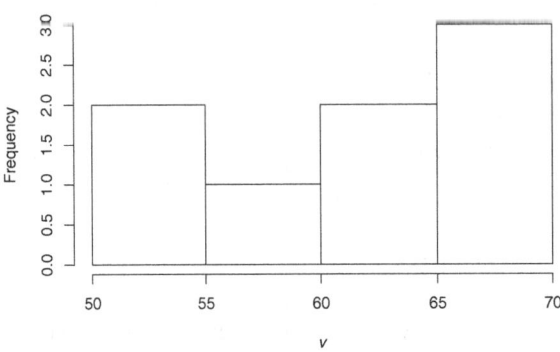

FIGURE 7.1 Histogram of a Vector

```
}  #                             End of Function
#------------------------------------------------------------------
```

Here is an example of using our cluster sampling function to select a cluster sample with four clusters from the database Hospital by the variable Hospital$region.

```
set.seed(1)
clustersHospital<-clusterSample(Hospital,Hospital$region,4)
```

## 7.2 Sampling Distribution of the Mean

The sample mean, $\bar{x}$, is a random variable because it changes when the sample changes. Figure 7.1 shows a histogram of the set of numbers in the following code fragment.

```
v<-c(54,55,59,63,64,68,69,70)
N<-length(v)
hist(v,main=NULL, xlab=expression(italic("v")))
```

Let us produce a set of samples of size 2 from the vector v defined above. Unlike the textbook example, our set of samples will be without repetition, just for simplicity. For instance, we do not include a pair like (1,1) and we take only one of the pairs (1,2) and (2,1). The number of such pairs is $\binom{N}{s}$, where $N$ is the number of elements in the population frame (vector v1 in our example) and $s$ is the size of the sample. In the

## 7.2. SAMPLING DISTRIBUTION OF THE MEAN

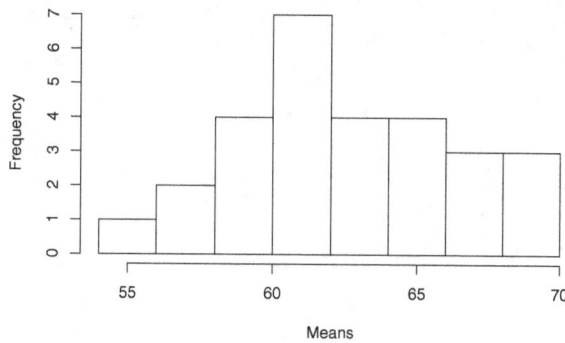

FIGURE 7.2 Histogram of Means

textbook example, the number of samples is $N^s$.

```
v<-c(54,55,59,63,64,68,69,70)
Nchoose2<-combn(v,2)
means=apply(Nchoose2,2,mean)
hist(means,main=NULL, xlab="Means")
```

The histogram in Figure 7.2 shows that the distribution of the sample means is closer to a normal distribution, although the population distribution is not.

Let us now reproduce the textbook Figure 7.4, which shows the histogram of a random sample of 5000 draws from a Poisson distribution. The result is shown in Figure 7.3.

```
set.seed(1)
x<-rpois(5000,1.3)
hist(rpois(5000,1.3),main=NULL, xlab=expression(italic("x")))
```

Using the Poisson "population" of 5000, we now construct 1000 subsamples of 500 elements each and calculate their means. The next figure reproduces Figure 7.5 in the textbook, suggesting that the sampling distribution of the mean approaches a normal distribution, although the population distribution is skewed.

This exercise is an illustration of the **central limit theorem**, which states that the sample mean of a population parameter is normally distributed irrespective of the distribution of the respective parameter in the population. The central limit theorem holds if the samples are sufficiently large; an empirical "rule" recommends samples of

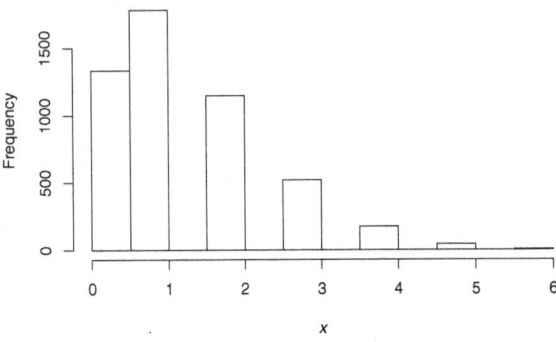

FIGURE 7.3 Histogram of a Poisson Distribution

at least 30 elements for the central limit theorem to work its magic.

```
set.seed(1)
x<-rpois(5000,1.3)
for(i in 1:1000){
  smpl<-sample(x,30,replace=TRUE)
  if(i==1){means<-mean(smpl)
  }else{means<-cbind(means,mean(smpl))}
}
hist(means,main=NULL, xlab="Means")
```

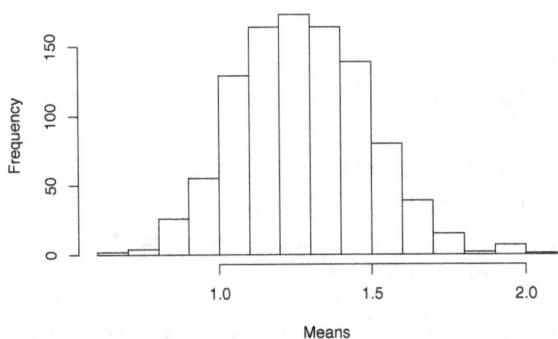

A mathematical result shows that the mean of a sampling distribution is equal to the population mean, which makes the sample mean an unbiased estimator of the population

## 7.3. SAMPLING DISTRIBUTION OF THE SAMPLE PROPORTION

mean. Another distribution parameter of the sample mean, its standard deviation, is equal to the population standard deviation divided by the square root of the sample size; the following formulas summarize these results, where $\bar{x}$ stands for the sample mean:

$$\mu_{\bar{x}} = \mu$$

$$\sigma_{\bar{x}} = \sigma/\sqrt{n}$$

**Demonstration Problem 7.1** Suppose $\mu = 448$, $\sigma = 21$, and $n = 49$. Calculate the probability $P(441 \leq \bar{x} \leq 446)$.

```
q1<-441
q2<-446
mu<-448
sigma<-21
n<-49
muxbar<-mu
sdxbar<-sigma/sqrt(n)
p1<-pnorm(q1,muxbar,sdxbar)
p2<-pnorm(q2,muxbar,sdxbar)
p<-p2-p1
p
```

```
## [1] 0.2426772
```

## 7.3 Sampling Distribution of the Sample Proportion

The **proportion** of a certain category in the sample is defined as

$$\hat{p} = x/n,$$

where $x$ is the size (number of elements) of the category in the sample and $n$ is the whole sample size. The sample proportion, $\bar{p}$, is also an unbiased estimator of the population proportion $p$. In other words, the mean of the sampling distribution of $\bar{p}$ is equal to $p$. The standard deviation of the sampling distribution of $\bar{p}$ is

$$\sigma_{\bar{p}} = \sqrt{\frac{pq}{n}},$$

where $q = 1 - p$. The central limit theorem applies to proportion if $np > 5$ and $nq > 5$.

**Demonstration Problem 7.3** If 10% of a population of parts is defective, what is the probability that 12 or more parts are defective in a random sample of 80? Since

$0.1 \times 80 > 5$, we can use a normal distribution for the sampling distribution of the proportion.

```
p<-0.1
n<-80
x<-12/80
muphat<-p
sdphat<-sqrt(p*(1-p)/n)
Pr<-pnorm(x,muphat,sdphat,lower.tail=FALSE)
Pr

## [1] 0.06801856
```

# Chapter 8

# Estimation for Single Populations

## 8.1 Estimating the Mean with z-Statistic

The z-statistic can be used to estimate the population mean $\mu$ when the variance of the population, $\sigma$, is known. In this case, a confidence interval for the mean is determined by the following formula:

$$\bar{x} - z_{\alpha/2}\frac{\sigma}{\sqrt{n}} \leq \mu \leq \bar{x} + z_{\alpha/2}\frac{\sigma}{\sqrt{n}}$$

*Demonstration Problem 8.1* Estimate the average numbers of years U.S. companies have been trading with companies in India.

```
n<-44
xbar<-10.455
sigma<-7.7
alpha<-0.1
zcr<-qnorm(alpha/2, lower.tail=FALSE)
lwb<-xbar-zcr*sigma/sqrt(n) # the lower bound of the CI
upb<-xbar+zcr*sigma/sqrt(n) # the upper bound of the CI
cat("Confidence interval = (",c(round(lwb,2),",",round(upb,2)),")")
```

## Confidence interval = ( 8.55 , 12.36 )

The TeachingDemos package in R provides the function z.test that performs hypothesis tests and calculates confidence levels for the mean when the population variance is known. The following code lines show how to use this function on the data in *Demonstration Problem 8.1*.

```
#install.packages("TeachingDemos")#if not installed
library(TeachingDemos)
confInterval<-z.test(xbar,stdev=sigma,alternative="two.sided",
     n=44,conf.level=0.9)
lwb1 <- confInterval$conf.int[1]
upb1 <- confInterval$conf.int[2]
cat("Confidence interval = (",c(round(lwb1,2),",",round(upb1,2)),")")

## Confidence interval = ( 8.55 , 12.36 )
```

## 8.2 Estimating the Mean with *t*-Statistic

The *t*-statistic is used when the standard deviation of a normally distributed population is not known and is replaced by the sample standard deviation, $s$. The *t*-statistic has a *t* distribution with $n-1$ degrees of freedom:

$$t = \frac{\bar{x} - \mu}{s/\sqrt{n}} \sim t_{n-1}$$

*Demonstration Problem 8.3* illustrates the use of the *t*-distribution to estimate the average numbers of days a piece of equipment is rented out per person per time. See the next code sequence.

```
dta<-c(3,1,3,2,5,1,2,1,4,2,1,3,1,1)
confLevel<-0.99
n <- length(dta)
df<-n-1
alpha<-1-confLevel
tcr<-qt(1-alpha/2,df)
xbar<-mean(dta)
s<-sd(dta)
lwb<-xbar-tcr*s/sqrt(n) #lower bound of the confidence interval
upb<-xbar+tcr*s/sqrt(n) #upper bound of the confidence interval
cat("Confidence interval = (",c(round(lwb,2),",",round(upb,2)),")")

## Confidence interval = ( 1.1 , 3.18 )
```

## 8.3. ESTIMATING THE POPULATION PROPORTION

Otherwise, one can use the t.test() function in the base R; as the next code shows, the result is the same.

```
dta<-c(3,1,3,2,5,1,2,1,4,2,1,3,1,1)
n <- 14
alpha<-0.01
ttst<-t.test(dta,alternative="two.sided",conf.level=confLevel)
lwb1<-ttst$conf.int[1]
upb1<-ttst$conf.int[2]
cat("Confidence interval = (",c(round(lwb1,2),",",round(upb1,2)),")")

## Confidence interval = ( 1.1 , 3.18 )
```

## 8.3 Estimating the Population Proportion

The confidence interval for proportion is determined with the formula

$$\hat{p} \pm z_{\alpha/2}\sqrt{\frac{\hat{p}\hat{q}}{n}}$$

where $\hat{p}$ is the sample proportion, $\hat{q} = 1 - \hat{p}$, $p$ is the population proportion, and $n$ is the sample size. While there are a few R functions to calculate this statistic, using various methods, one can use this formula directly in most cases. Let us construct a simple function, propCI() to apply the proportion confidence interval formula.

```
#------------------------------------------------------------------
#                   Function: Population Proportion
#------------------------------------------------------------------
propCI<-function(n,p_hat,conf.level){
alpha<-1-confLevel
zcr<-qnorm(1-alpha/2)
lwb<-p_hat-zcr*sqrt(p_hat*(1-p_hat)/n)
upb<-p_hat+zcr*sqrt(p_hat*(1-p_hat)/n)
lst=c(lwb,upb)
cat("Lower bound =",round(lwb,4),"; ",
    "Upper bound =",round(upb,4))
return(lst)
```

```
} #                          End of Function
#-------------------------------------------------------------
```

Let us apply the function propCI() on the data provided by the *Demonstration Problem 8.4*.

```
ci8.4<-propCI(210,.51,.92)
```

```
## Lower bound = 0.4211 ;  Upper bound = 0.5989
```

And, again, let us apply the new function to reproduce the results in the *Demonstration Problem 8.5*. As opposed to the *Demonstration Problem 8.4*, where we were given the proportion in the sample, the *Demonstration Problem 8.5* gives the number of observations in the category of interest in the sample. Thus, the second argument in the function propCI() should be the ratio of number in sample over sample size.

```
ci8.5<-propCI(423,72/423,.9)
```

```
## Lower bound = 0.1231 ;  Upper bound = 0.2173
```

## 8.4 Estimating the Population Variance

The sample variance, $s^2$, is an unbiased estimator of the population variance, and can be determined using the formula:

$$s^2 = \frac{\sum (x - \bar{x})^2}{n - 1}$$

This statistic has a $\chi^2$ distribution with $n-1$ degrees of freedom. The accuracy of this method depends crucially on the assumption of normal distribution in the population.

The formulas for a confidence interval of the variance reflect the asymmetric shape of the $\chi^2$ distribution.

$$\frac{(n-1)s^2}{\chi^2_{\alpha/2}} \leq \sigma^2 \leq \frac{(n-1)s^2}{\chi^2_{1-\alpha/2}}$$

$$df = n - 1$$

## 8.5. DETERMINING SAMPLE SIZE

where $n$ is the sample size, $s^2$ is the sample variance, and $1-\alpha$ is the confidence level.

```
#--------------------------------------------------------------------
#               Function: Confidence Interval for Variance
#--------------------------------------------------------------------
# Arguments: n=sample size, sVar=sample variance, confLevel
# Prints and returns CI limits
varCI<-function(n,sVar,confLevel){
  alpha<-1-confLevel
  chisq1<-qchisq(alpha/2,n-1,lower.tail=FALSE)
  chisq2<-qchisq(alpha/2,n-1)
  lwb<-(n-1)*sVar/chisq1
  upb<-(n-1)*sVar/chisq2
  lst<-c(lwb,upb)
  cat("Variance lower bound =",lwb)
  cat("\nVariance upper bound =",upb,"\n")
  return(lst)
} #                                     End of Function
#--------------------------------------------------------------------
```

Let us apply this function to the *Demonstration Problem 8.6*. The function prints the confidence interval bounds, but also returns them under the form of the list (*lower, upper*).

```
vci<-varCI(25,1.12^2,.95)

## Variance lower bound = 0.7647988
## Variance upper bound = 2.427646
```

## 8.5 Determining Sample Size

**Sample Size When Estimating $\mu$**

The formula is
$$n = \frac{z_{\alpha/2}^2 \sigma^2}{E^2},$$
where $n$ is the estimated sample size, $\sigma^2$ is the variance in the population, and $E$ is the desired error margin ($E = \bar{x} - \mu$). If $\sigma$ is not known, it can be considered equal to

a quarter of the range of the variable we study ($\sigma = range/4$).

```
#-----------------------------------------------------------------
#                  Function: Sample Size for Mean
#-----------------------------------------------------------------
# sigma=(1/4)*range if the population sigma is unknown
# var=sigma^2
sampleSizeM<-function(e,var,confLevel){
  alpha<-1-confLevel
  zcr<-qnorm(1-alpha/2)
  n<-zcr^2*var/e^2
  return(n)
} #                                     End of Function
#-----------------------------------------------------------------
```

The next code reproduces an example in *Section 8.5* of the textbook.

```
nMin<-sampleSizeM(1,var=16, confLevel=.9)
cat("Estimated sample size =",round(nMin,1))
```

```
## Estimated sample size = 43.3
```

And here the *Demonstration Problem 8.7* is reproduced, using the `sampleSize()` function again.

```
var=(.25*20)^2
nEstimated<-sampleSizeM(1,var,.95)
cat("Estimated sample size =",round(nEstimated,2))
```

```
## Estimated sample size = 96.04
```

**Sample Size When Estimating Proportion**

The formula is

$$n = \frac{z_{\alpha/2}^2 pq}{E^2},$$

where $p$ is the population proportion (unknown, but guessed from past experience or considered equal to 0.5), $q = 1 - p$, and $E$ is the desired margin of error in estimating the proportion, $E = \hat{p} - p$.

## 8.5. DETERMINING SAMPLE SIZE

```
#-------------------------------------------------------------
#                Function: Sample Size for Proportion
#-------------------------------------------------------------
# e is error, p is proportion (given, guessed, or taken =.5)
sampleSizeP<-function(e,p,confLevel){
  alpha<-1-confLevel
  zcr<-qnorm(1-alpha/2)
  n<-zcr^2*p*(1-p)/e^2
  return(n)
} #                              End of Function
#-------------------------------------------------------------
```

*Demonstration Problem 8.8*

```
nP<-sampleSizeP(.03,.4,.98)
cat("Sample size for proportion =",nP)
```

```
## Sample size for proportion = 1443.172
```

The textbook rounds the critical value of $z$ to two decimals, hence the slight difference in results.

# Chapter 9

# Hypothesis Testing: Single Populations

## 9.1 Population Mean, When Variance is Known

The test statistics for large samples (>30) in any population or for any sample in a normally distributed population is the same as before,

$$z = \frac{\bar{x} - \mu}{\sigma/\sqrt{n}}.$$

Let us reproduce the example in Section 9.2 (pages 276-278) in the textbook, which tests the hypothesis that the average income for CPAs is $98,000, with the sample size equal to 112, the population standard deviation of $14,530, the sample mean of $102,220, and a significance level $\alpha = 0.05$. The hypothesis to be tested is

$$H_0 : \mu = 98,500, \quad H_a : \mu \neq 98,500$$

```
h0<-98500
sd<-14530
alpha<-.05
n<-112
xbar<-102220
z<-(xbar-h0)/(sd/sqrt(n))
```

```
zcr<-qnorm(1-alpha/2)
cat("z-statistic =",round(z,2),", Critical z = ",round(zcr,2))
```

```
## z-statistic = 2.71 , Critical z =  1.96
```

Since the calculated $z$ exceeds the critical value, we reject the null hypothesis. For the same example let us calculate the $p$-value:

```
p<-2*(1-pnorm(z));p    # doubled because it is a two-tail test
```

```
## [1] 0.006738828
```

The test statistic formula needs a correction when the sample is less than 5% of the population, as follows:

$$z = \frac{\bar{x} - \mu}{\frac{\sigma}{\sqrt{n}}\sqrt{\frac{N-n}{N-1}}}$$

The **critical value method** asks what would be the sample mean that would make $z$ just equal to the critical $z$. For a two-sided test, the answer is given by the following formula:

$$\bar{x}_{cr} = \mu \pm z_{\alpha/2}\frac{\sigma}{\sqrt{n}}$$

```
lowxcr<-h0-zcr*sd/sqrt(n)
upxcr<-h0+zcr*sd/sqrt(n)
cat("lower x_cr =",lowxcr,"; upper x_cr =",upxcr,
    "; x_bar =",xbar)
```

```
## lower x_cr = 95809.06 ; upper x_cr = 101190.9 ; x_bar = 102220
```

The sample mean, $\bar{x}$, is above the upper limit, confirming our previous conclusion to reject the null hypothesis.

## 9.2 Population Mean, When Variance is Unknown

When the population standard deviation is unknown, we need to use a $t$-statistic instead of a $z$-statistic. The formula is the same as above, but with $\sigma$ replaced by $s$, the sample

## 9.3. TESTING HYPOTHESES ABOUT A PROPORTION

standard deviation. The $t$-statistic has a $t$-distribution with $n-1$ degrees of freedom. The population has to be normally distributed for any sample size.

$$t = \frac{\bar{x} - \mu}{\frac{s}{\sqrt{n}}}$$

The next lines of code reproduce the example in Section 9.3 of the textbook, where the hypothesis to be tested is

$$H_0 : \mu = 25, \quad H_a : \mu \neq 25$$

```
alpha<-.05
c<-25
x<-c(22.6,27.0,26.2,25.8,22.2,26.6,25.3,30.4,23.2,28.1,
     23.1,28.6,27.4,26.9,24.2,23.5,24.5,24.9,26.1,23.6)
n<-length(x)
xbar<-mean(x)
s<-sd(x)
df<-n-1
tcr<-qt(1-alpha/2,df)
t<-(xbar-c)/(s/sqrt(n))
cat("t = ",round(t,2),";   Critical t = ",round(tcr,2))
```

```
## t =  1.04 ;   Critical t =  2.09
```

Since $t < t_{cr}$, we cannot reject the null hypothesis. We reach the same conclusion if we use the $p$-value method, as follows:

```
p<-2*(1-pt(t,df))
cat("p-value/2 =",round(p/2,4),";   p-value = ",round(p,4))
```

```
## p-value/2 = 0.1557 ;   p-value =  0.3114
```

Since the $p$-value $> \alpha$, we cannot reject the null hypothesis.

## 9.3 Testing Hypotheses about a Proportion

As for confidence intervals, the test statistic for proportion is

$$z = \frac{\hat{p} - p}{\sqrt{\frac{pq}{n}}}$$

Let us reproduce the *Demonstration Problem 9.3*, which requires testing the hypothesis

$$H_0 : p = 0.17, \quad H_a : p > 0.17,$$

given $n = 116$, $\hat{p} = 116/550$, and $\alpha = 0.01$. Since this is a right-tail test, the rejection region is an area of magnitude $\alpha$ in the right tail of the $z$ distribution. For one-tail tests the *p*-values are not doubled, but directly compared to $\alpha$.

```
alpha<-0.01
n<-550 # sample size
ns<-116 # positives in sample
phat<-ns/n # sample proportion
p<-0.17 #hypothesized proportion
q<-1-p
z<-(phat-p)/sqrt(p*q/n) # calculated z
zcr<-qnorm(1-alpha) # critical z
pval<-1-pnorm(z) # p-value
cat("z = ",round(z,3),";  z_cr =",round(zcr,3),
    ";   p-value =",round(pval,3))
## z =  2.554 ;  z_cr = 2.326 ;   p-value = 0.005
```

We reject the null hypothesis, since $z > z_{cr}$; this result is confirmed by the *p*-value, since *p*-value $< \alpha$.

## 9.4 Testing Hypotheses about Variance

The test statistic for variance is very sensitive to violations of the assumption of a normally distributed population. Under this assumption, the test statistic is

$$\chi^2 = \frac{(n-1)s^2}{\sigma^2}$$

$$df = n - 1$$

Here is a reproduction of *Demonstration Problem 9.4*, which requires testing the (two-tail) hypothesis

$$H_0 : \sigma^2 = 25, \quad H_a : \sigma^2 \neq 25$$

The sample size is $n = 16$, the population variance is $\sigma^2 = 25$, and $\alpha = 0.1$.

## 9.5. TYPE II ERRORS

```
x<-c(57,46,48,63,56,53,51,53,52,44,55,51,44,44,48,50)
alpha<-.1
sig_sq<-25
n<-length(x)
df<-n-1
s_sq<-var(x)
chisq_cr1<-qchisq(alpha/2,df) # left-hand tail
chisq_cr2<-qchisq(1-alpha/2,df) # right-hand tail
chisqx<-(n-1)*s_sq/sig_sq
cat(" Lower critical chi_square =",chisq_cr1, "\n",
    "Upper critical chi_square =",chisq_cr2, "\n",
    "Test statistic chi_sq =",chisqx)
```

```
## Lower critical chi_square = 7.260944
## Upper critical chi_square = 24.99579
## Test statistic chi_sq = 16.8375
```

The test statistic falls in the non-rejection region.

## 9.5 Type II Errors

A **type II error** is the probability of not rejecting the null hypothesis when it is false and, therefore, it should be rejected. Let us first consider a hypothesis about the mean,

$$H_0 : \mu = \mu_0, \quad H_a : \mu \neq \mu_0$$

If $\bar{x}$ is the sample mean and $\mu$ is the true population mean, then the probability of a type II error is

$$Pr(t_1 \leq t \leq t_2),$$

where $t_1$ is the lower bound of the acceptance region of the true sampling distribution of the mean, and $t_2$ is the upper bound. These bounds can be calculated with the formulas:

$$t_1 = \frac{\mu_0 - \mu}{se(\mu_0)} - t_{cr}$$

$$t_2 = \frac{\mu_0 - \mu}{se(\mu_0)} + t_{cr}$$

In these equations, $t_{cr}$ corresponds to $\alpha/2$ for a two-tail test, and $\alpha$ for a one-tail test. A left-tail test will only use $t_1$; a right-tail test will only use $t_2$. Replace $t$ with $z$ when the population standard deviation is known.

# CHAPTER 9. HYPOTHESIS TESTING: SINGLE POPULATIONS

The function `type2z()`, shown in the next code box, calculates the probability of type II error for the mean. The function requires the following arguments:

- `alpha`, the significance level
- `sigma`, the population standard deviation
- `mu0`, the hypothesized mean
- `mu`, the true population mean
- `N`, the sample size
- `side`, the type of test, one of the following: "left," "two," or "right"

```
#-----------------------------------------------------------------
#                 Function: Type II Error for Mean
#-----------------------------------------------------------------
type2z<-function(alpha,sigma,mu0,mu,N,side){
  df<-N-1
  if(side=="left"){
    tcr<-qnorm(alpha)
    t1<-(mu0-mu)/(sigma/sqrt(N))+tcr
    beta<-1-pnorm(t1)
  } else if(side=="two"){
    tcr<-qnorm(1-alpha/2)
    t1<-(mu0-mu)/(sigma/sqrt(N))-tcr
    t2<-(mu0-mu)/(sigma/sqrt(N))+tcr
    beta<-pnorm(t2)-pnorm(t1)
  } else if(side=="right"){
    tcr<-qnorm(1-alpha)
    t2<-(mu0-mu)/(sigma/sqrt(N))+tcr
    beta<-pnorm(t2)
  }
return(beta)
} #                           End of Function
#-----------------------------------------------------------------
```

Let us apply this function to the example at page 301 of the textbook.

```
alpha <- 0.05
sigma<-0.1
mu0<-12
N<-60
mu<-11.99
beta11.99 <- type2z(alpha,sigma,mu0,mu,N,side="left")
```

## 9.5. TYPE II ERRORS

```
cat("Beta for mu=11.99 =",beta11.99)
```

## Beta for mu=11.99 = 0.80792

Here are two more examples, of which the first is the *Demonstration Problem 9.5*.

```
beta11.9<-type2z(alpha, sigma, mu0,mu=11.96,N,side="left")
cat("Beta in DP 9.5 =",beta11.9)
```

## Beta in DP 9.5 = 0.07303791

```
b<-type2z(0.05,21,20,28,49,"right")
cat("Beta =",b)
```

## Beta = 0.1534347

A function to calculate the **type II error for the proportion** follows the same procedure as the one for the mean, but with the standard deviation specific for the proportion,

$$z_c = \frac{\hat{p} - p}{\sqrt{\frac{pq}{n}}}$$

```
#-----------------------------------------------------------------
#           Function: Type II Error for Proportion
#-----------------------------------------------------------------
type2p<-function(alpha,phat,p,N,side){
  df<-N-1
  q<-1-p
  if(side=="left"){
    tcr<-qnorm(alpha)
    t1<-(phat-p)/sqrt(p*q/N)+tcr
    beta<-1-pnorm(t1)
  } else if(side=="two"){
    tcr<-qnorm(1-alpha/2)
    t1<-(phat-p)/sqrt(p*q/N)-tcr
    t2<-(phat-p)/sqrt(p*q/N)+tcr
    beta<-pnorm(t2)-pnorm(t1)
  } else if(side=="right"){
```

```
    tcr<-qnorm(1-alpha)
    t2<-(phat-p)/sqrt(p*q/N)+tcr
    beta<-pnorm(t2)
  }
return(beta)
} #                              End of Function
#-------------------------------------------------------------------
```

Let us apply the function `type2p` to *Demonstration Problem 9.6* (the slight difference in results appears because the textbook truncates intermediate results).

```
Betap<-type2p(0.05,.4,.36,250,"two")
cat("Beta for proportion =",Betap)
```

```
## Beta for proportion = 0.739153
```

## 9.6 Operating Characteristics and Power Curves

Table 9.5 (textbook) gives the probabilities of committing a type II error, $\beta$, as well as the power of the test, $1 - \beta$, for several values of the true mean in *Demonstration Problem 9.5*. Let us reproduce this table and draw the respective curves.

```
mean<-c(11.999,11.995,11.99,11.98,11.97,11.96,11.95)
Beta<-sapply(mean,type2z,alpha=.05,sigma=.1,mu0=12,N=60,
             side="left")
Power<-1-Beta
tbl<-data.frame(cbind(mean, Beta, Power));round(tbl,3)
```

```
##      mean  Beta Power
## 1 11.999 0.941 0.059
## 2 11.995 0.896 0.104
## 3 11.990 0.808 0.192
## 4 11.980 0.538 0.462
## 5 11.970 0.249 0.751
## 6 11.960 0.073 0.927
## 7 11.950 0.013 0.987
```

```
plot(mean,Beta,type="l", xlab="Mean")
```

## 9.6. OPERATING CHARACTERISTICS AND POWER CURVES

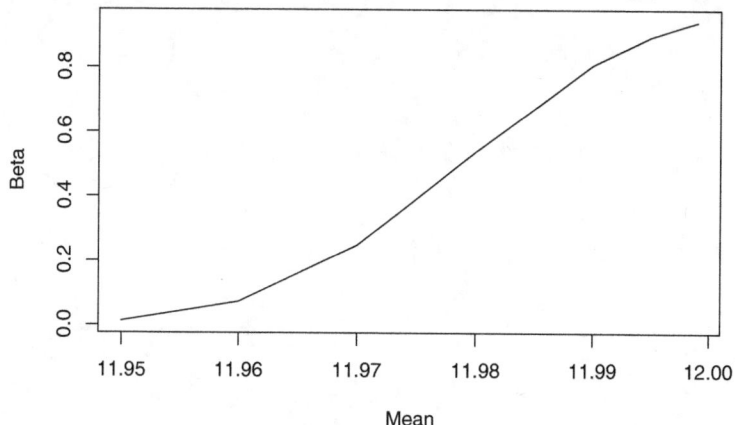

```
plot(mean,Power, type="l", xlab="Mean")
```

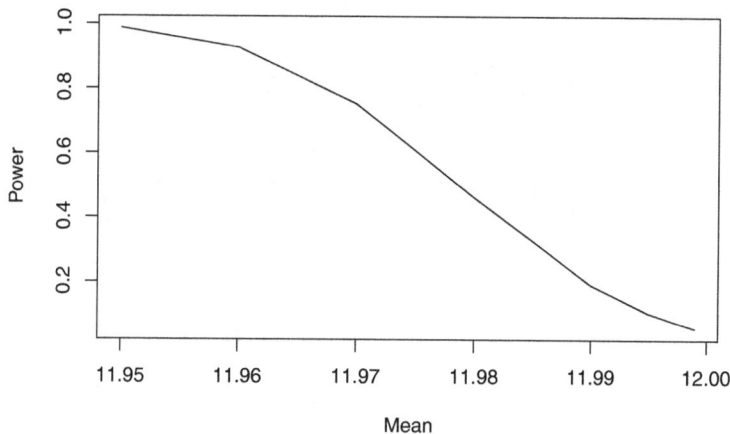

Please note the use of the function `sapply()` in the previous code lines. This function applies another function, in this case `type2z`, to a vector or a list of elements. The arguments of the `sapply()` function are: the vector to whose elements I wish to apply the function, the name of the function to be applied (without brackets), and the arguments of the function to be applied, except the one given before as a vector.

# Chapter 10

# Inferences about Two Populations

Unless otherwise stated, the methods in this chapter assume that the two populations to be compared are independent, such that the sample collected from one population does not influence in any way the sample from the other.

## 10.1 Difference in Two Means With Known Variance

The test statistic for the difference in two means when the samples are independent and the two population variances are known has a standard normal distribution and is given by the following formula. If the populations are normally distributed, this formula can be used for small samples as well.

$$z = \frac{(\bar{x}_1 - \bar{x}_2) - (\mu_1 - \mu_2)}{\sqrt{\frac{\sigma_1^2}{n_1} + \frac{\sigma_2^2}{n_2}}}$$

```
#-------------------------------------------------------------
#       Function: Difference in Means With Known Variance
#-------------------------------------------------------------
meanDiff<-function(n1,n2,xbar1,xbar2,sigma1,sigma2,
                   side,alpha=.05,delta=0){
z<-((xbar1-xbar2)-delta)/sqrt(sigma1^2/n1+sigma2^2/n2)
if(side=="left"){
   pvalue<-pnorm(z)
} else if (side=="two"){
```

```
      pvalue=2*(1-pnorm(abs(z)))
   } else if (side=="right"){
      pvalue=1-pnorm(z)
   }
diffbar<-xbar1-xbar2
lwb<-xbar1-xbar2-qnorm(1-alpha/2)*sqrt(sigma1^2/n1+sigma2^2/n2)
upb<-xbar1-xbar2+qnorm(1-alpha/2)*sqrt(sigma1^2/n1+sigma2^2/n2)
results<-list(pvalue,diffbar,lwb,upb)
names(results)<-c("pvalue","diffbar","lwb","upb")
return(results)
}#                      End of Function
#----------------------------------------------------------------
```

The function meanDiff() returns the $p$-value of a hypothesis test of the difference in means and a confidence interval. For the two-tail test, the function returns the $p$-value over both tails; therefore, this $p$-value should be compared to the whole value of $\alpha$, not to half of it. The argument side can take one of the following three values: "left" for a left-tail test, "right" for a right-tail test, and "two" for a two-tail test. If a value for $\alpha$ is not provided, it is automatically set to .05; if a value for $\delta$ is not provided, it is automatically set to 0, where $\delta$ is the hypothesized difference between the means. The difference in means is always $\bar{x}_1 - \bar{x}_2$.

Let us apply this function to the example at page 320, with $\delta = 0$.

```
alpha<-.05
n1<-32
n2<-34
delta<-0
xbar1<-70.7
xbar2<-62.187
sigma1<-16.253
sigma2<-12.9
side<-"two"
res<-meanDiff(n1,n2,xbar1,xbar2,sigma1,sigma2,
              side,alpha,delta)
cat("pvalue =",res$pvalue,"; diffbar =",res$diffbar,"\n",
    "lower bound =",res$lwb,"; upper bound =",res$upb)

## pvalue = 0.01889333 ; diffbar = 8.513
##  lower bound = 1.405755 ; upper bound = 15.62024
```

## 10.2. DIFFERENCE IN MEANS WITH UNKNOWN VARIANCES

Again, let us apply the meanDiff() function to *Demonstration Problem 10.1*.

```
res<-meanDiff(n1=87,n2=76,xbar1=3.352,xbar2=5.727,
     sigma1=1.1,sigma2=1.7,side="left",alpha=.01,delta=0)
cat("pvalue =",res$pvalue,"; diffbar =",res$diffbar,"\n",
    "lower bound =",res$lwb,"; upper bound =",res$upb)

## pvalue = 9.875508e-26 ; diffbar = -2.375
##  lower bound = -2.962009 ; upper bound = -1.787991
```

The next code lines reproduce the example at page 324.

```
res<-meanDiff(n1=60,n2=80,xbar1=5.84,xbar2=2.67,
     sigma1=1.41,sigma2=0.54,side="two",alpha=.02,delta=0)
cat("pvalue =",res$pvalue,"; diffbar =",res$diffbar,"\n",
    "lower bound =",res$lwb,"; upper bound =",res$upb)

## pvalue = 0 ; diffbar = 3.17
##  lower bound = 2.72385 ; upper bound = 3.61615
```

## 10.2 Difference in Means with Unknown Variances

As before, we assume that the two samples are independent and the variable in question is normally distributed in the populations. Since the variances are unknown, we need to replace them by sample variances, which changes the sampling distribution. The test statistic and the formula for degrees of freedom depend on whether we can assume that the two populations have equal variances.

**Equal Variances**

The number of degrees of freedom of the test statistic distribution is given by

$$df = n_1 + n_2 - 2.$$

The test statistic formula is

$$t = \frac{(\bar{x}_1 - \bar{x}_2) - (\mu_1 - \mu_2)}{\sqrt{\frac{s_1^2(n_1-1)+s_2^2(n_2-1)}{n_1+n_2-2}}\sqrt{\frac{1}{n_1}+\frac{1}{n_2}}}.$$

**Unequal Variances**

$$df = \frac{\left(\frac{s_1^2}{n_1} + \frac{s_2^2}{n_2}\right)^2}{\frac{\left(\frac{s_1^2}{n_1}\right)^2}{n_1-1} + \frac{\left(\frac{s_2^2}{n_2}\right)^2}{n_2-1}}$$

$$t = \frac{(\bar{x}_1 - \bar{x}_2) - \mu_1 - \mu_2}{\sqrt{\frac{s_1^2}{n_1} + \frac{s_2^2}{n_2}}}$$

The function meanDiffs() is very similar to meanDiff(), except it uses the $t$-distribution instead of the standard normal and calculates the number of degrees of freedom as for populations with different, but unknown variances. The function tests the hypothesis $H_0 : \mu_1 - \mu_2 = 0$ against the appropriate alternative for a left, right, or two-tail test; the argument side specifies, as before, the type of test that the researcher desires. In addition, the function delivers a confidence interval for $\delta$, the difference in means. If the sample data are given for the two samples instead of their variances, variances can be calculated using the R function var(), or sd() if you wish to calculate directly the standard deviations.

```
#------------------------------------------------------------
#     Function: Difference in Means With Unknown Variance
#------------------------------------------------------------
meanDiffs<-
  function(n1,n2,xbar1,xbar2,s1,s2,side,alpha=.05,delta=0){
t<-((xbar1-xbar2)-delta)/sqrt(s1^2/n1+s2^2/n2)
df<-(s1^2/n1+s2^2/n2)^2/((s1^2/n1)^2/(n1-1)+(s2^2/n2)^2/(n2-1))
if(side=="left"){
   pvalue<-pt(t,df)
} else if (side=="two"){
   pvalue=2*(1-pt(abs(t),df))
} else if (side=="right"){
   pvalue=1-pt(t,df)
}
diffbar<-xbar1-xbar2
lwb<-xbar1-xbar2-qt(1-alpha/2,df)*sqrt(s1^2/n1+s2^2/n2)
upb<-xbar1-xbar2+qt(1-alpha/2,df)*sqrt(s1^2/n1+s2^2/n2)
res<-list(pvalue,diffbar,lwb,upb)
names(res)<-c("pvalue","diffbar","lwb","upb")
return(res)
}#                        End of Function
#------------------------------------------------------------
```

## 10.2. DIFFERENCE IN MEANS WITH UNKNOWN VARIANCES

The next exercise is an application of the *difference in means* function to the example at page 329 in the textbook.

```
n1<-15; n2<-12
xbar1<-47.73; xbar2<-56.5
s1<-sqrt(19.459); s2<-sqrt(18.273)
delta<-0
side<-"two"
alpha<-.05
res<-meanDiffs(n1,n2,xbar1,xbar2,s1,s2,side,alpha,delta)
cat("pvalue =",res$pvalue,"; diffbar =",res$diffbar,"\n",
    "lower bound =",res$lwb,"; upper bound =",res$upb)

## pvalue = 2.361007e-05 ; diffbar = -8.77
##  lower bound = -12.23569 ; upper bound = -5.304308
```

When we know the data for the two populations, we can use R's function `t.test()` for the difference in means, as follows (see the example at page 329 in the textbook):

```
a<-c(56,47,42,50,47,51,52,53,42,44,45,43,52,48,44)
b<-c(59,52,53,54,57,56,55,64,53,65,53,57)
t.test(a,b)

##
##   Welch Two Sample t-test
##
## data:  a and b
## t = -5.2182, df = 24.034, p-value = 2.384e-05
## alternative hypothesis: true difference in means is not equal to 0
## 95 percent confidence interval:
##  -12.233762  -5.299571
## sample estimates:
## mean of x mean of y
##  47.73333  56.50000
```

The R function `t.test()` operates on one or two samples. As with any other function, the missing arguments in the call line will have the default values specified in the syntax of the function. The `t.test()` function accepts the following arguments:

- x, a vector of data
- y, an optional second vector of data, required when a difference in means is being tested

- alternative, the type of alternative hypothesis; it can be one of the following: "two-sided," "greater," or "less"
- mu, the hypothesized value of the mean or the hypothesized difference in means.
- var.equal, a logical variable; if TRUE, the variances in the two populations are assumed equal
- conf.level, the desired confidence level of the interval; if missing, it is considered 0.95

## 10.3 Two Related Sample $t$-Test

Different authors may refer to this test by other terminology, such as *dependent samples*, or *matched-pairs*, *related measures*, or *correlated* $t$-test. Testing treatment effects (before–after) on the same objects or persons is an example of a two related sample situation. R uses the same t.test() function as before, but with the argument paired=TRUE. The following code reproduces *Demonstration Problem 10.5*.

```
before<-c(32,11,21,17,30,38,14)
after<-c(39,15,35,13,41,39,22)
t.test(before,after,alternative="less",paired=TRUE)

##
##   Paired t-test
##
## data:  before and after
## t = -2.5427, df = 6, p-value = 0.02196
## alternative hypothesis: true difference in means is less than 0
## 95 percent confidence interval:
##        -Inf -1.381023
## sample estimates:
## mean of the differences
##                -5.857143
```

## 10.4 Differences in Population Proportions

R provides the function prop.test() to test hypotheses of equal or given proportions. Its syntax is as follows:

## 10.4. DIFFERENCES IN POPULATION PROPORTIONS

```
prop.test(x, n, p=NULL, alternative=c("two.sided", "less", "greater"),
conf.level=0.95, correct=TRUE)
```

where x is a vector of counts of successes, or a table with two columns, or a matrix; n is a vector of counts of trials, which is ignored if x is a matrix or a table; p is a vector of probabilities of success, of the same length as x.

The next code fragment reproduces the example at page 349.

```
trials<-c(755,616) # these are n1 and n2 in the text
successes<-trials*c(.57,.5)
prop.test(x=successes,n=trials,alternative="greater",correct=FALSE)

##
##  2-sample test for equality of proportions without continuity
##  correction
##
## data:  successes out of trials
## X-squared = 6.6886, df = 1, p-value = 0.004852
## alternative hypothesis: greater
## 95 percent confidence interval:
##  0.0255439 1.0000000
## sample estimates:
## prop 1 prop 2
##   0.57   0.50
```

**Caution:** For a two-sided test, the $p$-value calculated by R is twice as much as the one in the textbook; therefore, it should be compared to $\alpha$, not to $\alpha/2$.

```
trials<-c(100,95) # these are n1 and n2 in the text
successes<-c(24,39)
prop.test(x=successes,n=trials,alternative="two.sided",correct=FALSE)

##
##  2-sample test for equality of proportions without continuity
##  correction
##
## data:  successes out of trials
## X-squared = 6.4778, df = 1, p-value = 0.01092
## alternative hypothesis: two.sided
## 95 percent confidence interval:
##  -0.30011107 -0.04094156
```

```
## sample estimates:
##    prop 1    prop 2
## 0.2400000 0.4105263
```

Here is the example at page 352, which seeks to calculate a 98% confidence interval for the difference in two proportions.

```
trials<-c(400,480) # these are n1 and n2 in the text
successes<-c(48,187)
prop.test(x=successes,n=trials,alternative="two.sided",
        conf.level=.98,correct=FALSE)
```

```
## 
##  2-sample test for equality of proportions without continuity
##  correction
## 
## data:  successes out of trials
## X-squared = 81.011, df = 1, p-value < 2.2e-16
## alternative hypothesis: two.sided
## 98 percent confidence interval:
##  -0.3336924 -0.2054742
## sample estimates:
##    prop 1    prop 2
## 0.1200000 0.3895833
```

## 10.5 Testing Two Population Variances

The test statistic for the ratio of two populations is the $F$-value

$$F = \frac{s_1^2}{s_2^2}$$

```
#--------------------------------------------------------
#       Function: Two Population Variance Test
#--------------------------------------------------------
varDiff<-function(n1,n2,var1,var2,side,alpha){
df1<-n1-1
df2<-n2-1
fRatio<-var1/var2
if(side=="left"){
```

## 10.5. TESTING TWO POPULATION VARIANCES

```
      pvalue<-pf(fRatio,df1,df2)
      crF_left<-qf(alpha, df1,df2)
      crF_right<-NA
    } else if (side=="two"){
      pvalue=2*(1-pf(fRatio,df1,df2))
      crF_right<-qf(1-alpha/2,df1,df2)
      crF_left<-qf(alpha/2,df1,df2)
    } else if (side=="right"){
      pvalue=pf(fRatio,df1,df2,lower.tail=FALSE)
      crF_right<-qf(1-alpha,df1,df2)
      crF_left<-NA
    }
retlist<-c(fRatio,pvalue, crF_left,crF_right)
names(retlist)<-c("F-ratio","p-value","crF_left","crF_right")
return(retlist)
}#                End of Function
#---------------------------------------------------------------
```

Let us now apply the new function, varDiff(), to the right-tail test in the example at page 358.

```
var1<-.11378
var2<-.02023
n1<-10
n2<-12
side<-"right"
res<-varDiff(n1,n2,var1,var2,side=side, alpha=0.05);
round(res,4)
```

```
##    F-ratio  p-value  crF_left  crF_right
##     5.6243   0.0047        NA     2.8962
```

The base R function (the one that comes with the base installation of R) for testing the variances of two samples is

```
var.test(x,  y,  ratio=1,  alternative=c("two.sided",    "less",
"greater"), conf.level = 0.95, ...),
```

where x and y are vectors of data and ratio is the hypothesized variance ratio. If ratio is 1, then it can be omitted from the list of arguments; conf.level can be omitted if it is equal to 0.95.

I reproduce here the example at page 356, which is a two-sided test of equality of variances (ratio= 1).

```
x1<-c(22.3,21.8,22.3,21.6,21.8,21.9,22.4,22.5,
      22.2,21.6)
x2<-c(22.0,22.1,21.8,21.9,22.2,22.0,21.7,21.9,
      22.0,22.1,21.9,22.1)
tst<-var.test(x1,x2,ratio=1,alternative="two.sided")
tst
```

```
##
##  F test to compare two variances
##
## data:  x1 and x2
## F = 5.625, num df = 9, denom df = 11, p-value = 0.009387
## alternative hypothesis: true ratio of variances is not equal to 1
## 95 percent confidence interval:
##   1.567761 22.005297
## sample estimates:
## ratio of variances
##           5.624969
```

The next code fragment reproduces the *Demonstration Problem 10.7*, which requires a right-sided test of variances,

$$H_0 : \sigma_1^2 = \sigma_2^2, \quad H_a : \sigma_1^2 > \sigma_2^2$$

```
x1a<-c(18500,19250,16400,20750,17600,21800,14750)
x2a<-c(23000,21900,22500,21200,21000,22800,23100,21300)
var.test(x1,x2,alternative="greater")
```

```
##
##  F test to compare two variances
##
## data:  x1 and x2
## F = 5.625, num df = 9, denom df = 11, p-value = 0.004693
## alternative hypothesis: true ratio of variances is greater than 1
## 95 percent confidence interval:
##   1.942174      Inf
## sample estimates:
## ratio of variances
```

## 10.5. TESTING TWO POPULATION VARIANCES

```
##              5.624969
```

Let us do another test for our `varDiff()` function: Let us solve the example at page 359.

```
var1a<-var(x1a)
var2a<-var(x2a)
varDiff(7,8,var1a,var2a,"right",.01)
```

```
##       F-ratio      p-value    crF_left    crF_right
## 8.087209302  0.007167222          NA  7.191404785
```

# Chapter 11

# Analysis of Variance

Independent variables that take discrete values are called *levels*, or *classifications*. To analyze such data, a researcher can use the *analysis of variance* technique (aka *ANOVA*).

## 11.1 One-Way ANOVA

A **completely randomized design** is an experimental design where subjects are randomly assigned to one of the several *treatment* groups. Such an experiment involves only one independent variable, which can be of several categories.

Example: Measurements of a valve opening, when valves have been produced by four different operators. The dependent variable is valve opening, and the independent variable is the operator's identifier (1, 2, 3, or 4). We would like to determine if there is a significant difference in the means of the four categories.

Why not to do pair-wise $t$-tests for the equality of means? Because, for the second and the subsequent tests, the significance level changes. If it was $\alpha = 0.05$ for the first $t$-test, it increases every time we do another test.

ANOVA tests a joint hypothesis; if $k$ samples are tested, the hypothesis is

$$H_0 : \mu_1 = \mu_2 = ... = \mu_k$$

$H_a$ : At least one of the means is different from zero

The aov() function in R returns SSC (the column sum of squares) and SSE (the error sum of squares). It requires, however, the data under the form of a data frame of which one of the columns is the variable measured (the dependent variable) and another column is the category variable. The data frame may contain other variables too.

The example at page 377 gives the valve openings for four groups of operators in a table with columns of unequal lengths. A data frame does not accept vectors of different lengths (or, more precisely, expands the shorter vectors); lists, on the other hand, accept elements of different lengths. Thus, to re-shape the data as aov() requires, I will gather the four columns into a list, then apply the function stack(), which turns the list into a data frame compatible with aov().

In this example, I demonstrate how to apply three functions: aov(), which gives the sums of squares, one.way(), which calculates the $F$-statistic for the equality of means, and TukeyHSD(), which calculates a confidence interval for each category. The simple TukeyHSD() should only be applied to balanced data, where categories have an equal number of observations. Finally, the plot() function shows the confidence intervals in one graph.

```
op1<-c(6.33,6.26,6.31,6.29,6.4)# Valve openings, Operator 1
op2<-c(6.26,6.36,6.23,6.27,6.19,6.5,6.19,6.22)
op3<-c(6.44,6.38,6.58,6.54,6.56,6.34,6.58)
op4<-c(6.29,6.23,6.19,6.21)
lst<-list(i1=op1,i2=op2,i3=op3,i4=op4)
stk<-stack(lst)
a<-aov(values~ind,data=stk);a
```

```
## Call:
##    aov(formula = values ~ ind, data = stk)
##
## Terms:
##                         ind  Residuals
## Sum of Squares    0.2365801  0.1549157
## Deg. of Freedom           3         20
##
## Residual standard error: 0.08801015
## Estimated effects may be unbalanced
```

```
oneway.test(values~ind,data=stk)
```

```
##
##  One-way analysis of means (not assuming equal variances)
##
```

## 11.1. ONE-WAY ANOVA

```
## data:  values and ind
## F = 10.697, num df = 3.000, denom df = 10.786, p-value = 0.001454
```

The *Demonstration Problem 11.2* analyzes the tensile strength of a metal under five levels of temperature. Since this is a balanced experimental design, we can use the TukeyHSD() function.

```
t1<-c(2.46,2.41,2.43,2.47,2.46)
t2<-c(2.38,2.34,2.31,2.4,2.32)
t3<-c(2.51,2.48,2.46,2.49,2.5)
t4<-c(2.49,2.47,2.48,2.46,2.44)
t5<-c(2.56,2.57,2.53,2.55,2.55)
lst<-list(i1=t1,i2=t2,i3=t3,i4=t4,i5=t5)
stk<-stack(lst)
a<-aov(values~ind,data=stk);a
```

```
## Call:
##    aov(formula = values ~ ind, data = stk)
##
## Terms:
##                       ind   Residuals
## Sum of Squares    0.108024   0.012360
## Deg. of Freedom          4         20
##
## Residual standard error: 0.02485961
## Estimated effects may be unbalanced
```

```
oneway.test(values~ind,data=stk)
```

```
##
##  One-way analysis of means (not assuming equal variances)
##
## data:  values and ind
## F = 36.034, num df = 4.000, denom df = 9.826, p-value = 7.533e-06
```

```
tk<-TukeyHSD(a,conf.level=0.99)
tk
```

```
##   Tukey multiple comparisons of means
##     99% family-wise confidence level
##
## Fit: aov(formula = values ~ ind, data = stk)
##
```

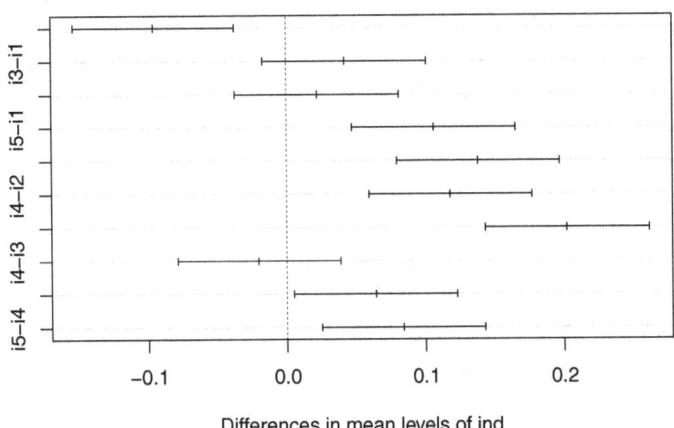

FIGURE 11.1 One-Way ANOVA

```
## $ind
##             diff         lwr         upr       p adj
## i2-i1     -0.096 -0.154848019 -0.03715198 0.0000513
## i3-i1      0.042 -0.016848019  0.10084802 0.0945606
## i4-i1      0.022 -0.036848019  0.08084802 0.6350992
## i5-i1      0.106  0.047151981  0.16484802 0.0000133
## i3-i2      0.138  0.079151981  0.19684802 0.0000003
## i4-i2      0.118  0.059151981  0.17684802 0.0000028
## i5-i2      0.202  0.143151981  0.26084802 0.0000000
## i4-i3     -0.020 -0.078848019  0.03884802 0.7105037
## i5-i3      0.064  0.005151981  0.12284802 0.0048087
## i5-i4      0.084  0.025151981  0.14284802 0.0002737
```

plot(tk)

The resulting graph, which is displayed in Figure 11.1, shows the confidence intervals based on pair-wise comparisons, for which the TukeyHSD() function also provides $p$-values.

**The Tukey–Kramer procedure** applies when the samples are of unequal sizes, where the simple TukeyHSD() function is not appropriate. The DTK package provides such a possibility. The sequence of using the DTK package is as follows: first create a vector that includes all the samples; then create a factor vector, which contains an indicator for each of your samples; then apply the function DTK.test and DTK.plot to plot

## 11.1. ONE-WAY ANOVA

pair-wise comparisons between samples; finally, apply the TK.test() function for the Tukey–Kramer test of differences in means.

```
# install.packages(DTK) #if not installed
library(DTK)
alpha<-0.05
nsamples=4 # the number of samples
data.vector<-c(op1,op2,op3,op4)
lengths<-c(5,8,7,4) #sample sizes, in the same order as data.vector
factor.vector<-gl.unequal(n=nsamples,k=lengths)#the factor vector
dtktest<-DTK.test(data.vector,factor.vector,alpha)
DTK.plot(dtktest)
```

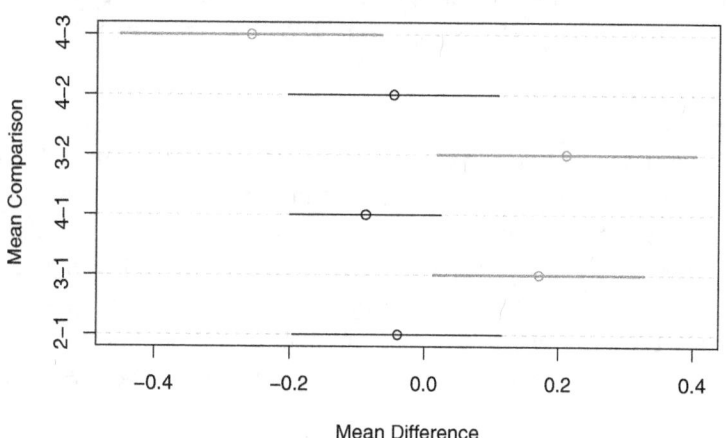

```
tktest<-TK.test(data.vector,factor.vector,alpha)
tktest

##    Tukey multiple comparisons of means
##       95% family-wise confidence level
##
## Fit: aov(formula = x ~ f)
##
## $f
##              diff         lwr         upr      p adj
## 2-1   -0.0405000  -0.18093243  0.09993243  0.8502854
```

```
## 3-1   0.1705714  0.02633255   0.31481031 0.0169205
## 4-1  -0.0880000 -0.25324639   0.07724639 0.4613461
## 3-2   0.2110714  0.08358107   0.33856179 0.0008519
## 4-2  -0.0475000 -0.19834863   0.10334863 0.8144408
## 4-3  -0.2585714 -0.41296992  -0.10417294 0.0007541
```

The graph shows that the pairs 3–1, 3–2, and 4–3 have significantly different means, which is confirmed by the low $p$-values in the TK test output.

## 11.2 The Randomized Block Design

The randomized block design accounts for additional factors that may influence the outcome of an experiment. The main factor of interest to the researcher, the "treatment" factor, is arranged in columns; the control, or "block" factor is arranged in rows. In the example of investigating if tires wear differently at different speeds (page 397 in the textbook), speed is the treatment, or column factor, while supplier is the block, or row factor. The numbers in the table represent wear, the measurement (or dependent) variable.

The function performing a randomized block analysis in R is aov(), which requires a formula of the form dependent variable ~ treatment factor + block factor. The researcher needs to create the two factor variables, treatment and block, and to re-arrange the measurement variable together with the two factor variables (speed and suppliers) in a long table before applying the aov() function. The long table will have three columns: measurement variable, treatment factor, and block factor; the number of rows in the long table is equal to the total number of measurements. Thus, each row in our long table will show a value for wear and its corresponding speed and supplier.

This re-shaping of the data table can be performed using the factor-generating function gl(), with the following arguments:

- number of levels of the factor variable (speeds or suppliers)
- number of replications of a level of the factor
- total number of observations (the length of the factor variable)
- an optional vector of labels, one for each level

(In the following code fragment, the "long" table is not actually formed; instead, its three columns are called together in the function aov.)

```
slow<-c(3.7,3.4,3.5,3.2,3.9)# wear for speed='slow,' all suppliers
medium<-c(4.5,3.9,4.1,3.5,4.8)#wear for speed='medium,' all suppliers
```

## 11.2. THE RANDOMIZED BLOCK DESIGN

```
fast<-c(3.1,2.8,3.0,2.6,3.4)  # wear for speed='fast,' all suppliers
k<-3 # number of columns in the initial table (speed levels)
n<-5 # number of rows in the initial table (blocks, or suppliers)
tot<-n*k # total number of observations
treat<-gl(k,1,tot)# the 'speed' indicator (factor) variable
block<-gl(n,k,tot)# the 'supplier' indicator (factor) variable
wear<-c(rbind(slow,medium,fast)) #the 'long' wear vector
anov<-aov(wear~treat+block)
sanov<-summary(anov) #the summary shows more information
sanov
```

```
##             Df Sum Sq Mean Sq F value   Pr(>F)
## treat        2  3.484  1.7420   97.68 2.39e-06 ***
## block        4  1.549  0.3873   21.72 0.000236 ***
## Residuals    8  0.143  0.0178
## ---
## Signif. codes:  0 '***' 0.001 '**' 0.01 '*' 0.05 '.' 0.1 ' ' 1
```

The output generated by aov() shows degrees of freedom, sums of squares, $F$-values, and $p$-values, testing the hypothesis that the means of the treatments are equal. In our case, the $p$-value of the treat factor is virtually 0, rejecting the hypothesis that tires wear is the same at the three levels of speed investigated.

Since the structure of the aov() output is not very transparent, it may help to see a few examples of how to retrieve some of the information stored in the summary aov() object. See the next code lines.

```
sanov<-summary(anov)
dfSpeed<-sanov[[1]][1,1]  # the "column" degrees of freedom
FSpeed<-sanov[[1]][1,4]   # the F-value of the treatment factor
SSC<-sanov[[1]][1,2]      # the SSC
cat(" Treatment (Speed) DF =",dfSpeed,"\n",
    "Treatment F-value =",FSpeed,"\n",
    "Treatment SS, SSC =",SSC)
```

```
##  Treatment (Speed) DF = 2
##  Treatment F-value = 97.68224
##  Treatment SS, SSC = 3.484
```

Let us replicate the *Demonstration Problem 11.3* using the same randomized block procedure as above.

```
miami<-c(3.47,3.43,3.44,3.46,3.46,3.44)
philadelphia<-c(3.40,3.41,3.41,3.45,3.40,3.43)
minneapolis<-c(3.38,3.42,3.43,3.40,3.39,3.42)
sanantonio<-c(3.32,3.35,3.36,3.30,3.39,3.39)
oakland<-c(3.50,3.44,3.45,3.45,3.48,3.49)
k<-5 # treatment categories = number of columns
n<-6 # control, or block categories
N<-k*n
price<-c(rbind(miami,philadelphia,minneapolis,sanantonio,oakland))
treatment<-gl(k,1,N)
block<-gl(n,k,N)
anov<-aov(price~treatment+block)
sanov<-summary(anov)
sanov
##             Df  Sum Sq  Mean Sq  F value  Pr(>F)
## treatment    4 0.04851 0.012128   18.941 1.41e-06 ***
## block        5 0.00203 0.000405    0.633    0.677
## Residuals   20 0.01281 0.000640
## ---
## Signif. codes:  0 '***' 0.001 '**' 0.01 '*' 0.05 '.' 0.1 ' ' 1
```

The $p$-values suggest that the average prices in the five geographic regions are not equal, but there are no significant differences in average prices across brands.

## 11.3 Two-Way ANOVA

Factorial design involves two or more *treatments*, or independent variables, with every treatment considered under every level of the other treatments. The advantage of factorial design is that confounding factors can be controlled within the experiment, thus increasing the power of the experiment. A factorial design tests three hypotheses: row means are equal, column means are equal, and the interaction effects are zero. We only examine factorial designs with two treatments, but the method can easily be extended to more than two treatments.

The following code reproduces an example in the textbook (page 406), where one of the four numbers (ratings) measure the importance of "availability of profitable investment opportunities" in CEOs' opinions; a set of four such ratings are given for each combination of the treatment levels. One treatment variable (how stockholders are informed) has two levels (rows), and the other (where company stock is traded)

## 11.3. TWO-WAY ANOVA

has three levels. Thus, the data comes in a $2 \times 5$ partitioned matrix in which each entry is a vector with four elements (the ratings).

```
X11<-c(2,1,2,1) # four ratings for informed=1 and location=1
X12<-c(2,3,3,2) # four ratings for informed=1 and location=2
X13<-c(4,3,4,3) # four ratings for informed=1 and location=3
X21<-c(2,3,1,2) # four ratings for informed=2 and location=1
X22<-c(3,3,2,4) # four ratings for informed=2 and location=2
X23<-c(4,4,3,4) # four ratings for informed=2 and location=3
m<-4 # number of ratings
n<-2 # number of 'informed'
k<-3 # number of 'locations'
N<-m*n*k # total number of observations (ratings)
X<-c(rbind(X11,X12,X13,X21,X22,X23))
row<-gl(n,k,N) # vector of indicators for the row treatment
col<-gl(k,1,N) # vector of indicators for the column treatment
anov<-aov(X~row*col)
sanov<-summary(anov)
sanov
```

```
##              Df Sum Sq Mean Sq F value  Pr(>F)
## row           1  1.042   1.042   2.419   0.137
## col           2 14.083   7.042  16.355 8.95e-05 ***
## row:col       2  0.083   0.042   0.097   0.908
## Residuals    18  7.750   0.431
## ---
## Signif. codes:  0 '***' 0.001 '**' 0.01 '*' 0.05 '.' 0.1 ' ' 1
```

The results show a small $p$-value for columns, which indicates a significant effect of where a company's stock is traded; on the other hand, neither the row treatment variable, nor the interaction terms have a significant effect on a CEO's rating on profitable investment opportunities (the variable "rating").

The following code fragment replicates *Demonstration Problem 11.4*. Unlike in the previous example, I introduced the measurement vector all at once, following the sequence vector–column–row. The same sequence needs to be considered when creating the factor variables `col` and `row`, such that the combination of these two factors correctly places each observation in its row and column.

```
x<-c(3,4.5,4,    2,2.5,2,     2.5,1,1.5,   # days of absence
     5,4.5,4,    1,3,2.5,     0,1.5,2,
     2.5,3,3.5,  1,3,1.5,     3.5,3.5,4,
     2,2,3,      5,4.5,2.5,   4,4.5,5)
m<-3 # observations per treatment pair
n<-4 # row treatment levels (type of warehouse)
k<-3 # column treatment levels (length of training period)
N<-m*n*k # total number of observations
row<-gl(n,m*k,N)
col<-gl(k,m,N)
```

Here is the long-table representation of the measurement vector and the treatment factor indicators.

```
head(data.frame(cbind(x,row,col)),n=12)
```

```
##       x row col
## 1   3.0   1   1
## 2   4.5   1   1
## 3   4.0   1   1
## 4   2.0   1   2
## 5   2.5   1   2
## 6   2.0   1   2
## 7   2.5   1   3
## 8   1.0   1   3
## 9   1.5   1   3
## 10  5.0   2   1
## 11  4.5   2   1
## 12  4.0   2   1
```

Once we are sure that the indicator vectors are correct, we can do the ANOVA calculations.

```
anov<-aov(x~row*col)
summary(anov)
```

```
##              Df Sum Sq Mean Sq F value   Pr(>F)
## row           3   6.41   2.137   3.457   0.0322 *
## col           2   5.01   2.507   4.056   0.0304 *
## row:col       6  33.15   5.525   8.940 3.54e-05 ***
## Residuals    24  14.83   0.618
## ---
```

## 11.3. TWO-WAY ANOVA

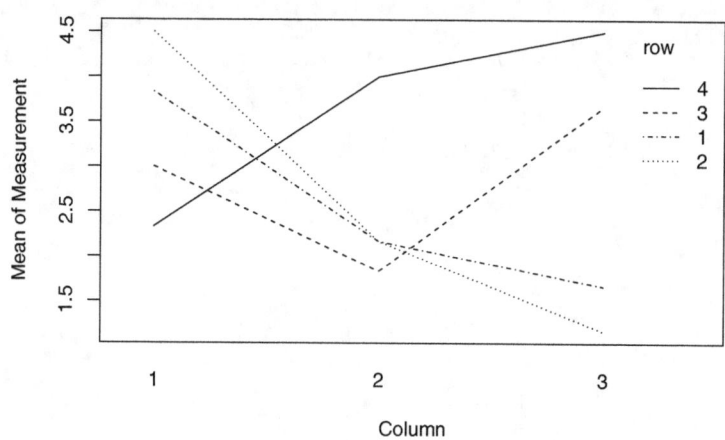

FIGURE 11.2 Averages of Measurement

```
## Signif. codes:  0 '***' 0.001 '**' 0.01 '*' 0.05 '.' 0.1 ' ' 1
```

Next, we can create a graph (Figure 11.2) to show the averages of the measurement, x, with respect to the two treatment variables, as follows:

```
interaction.plot(x.factor=col,trace.factor=row,response=x,
                 ylab="Mean of Measurement", xlab="Column")
```

# Chapter 12

# Simple Regression Analysis and Correlation

The R function cor() calculates correlations; by default, it uses the Pearson method described in the textbook. Please consult the description of this function when other methods are required. The following example calculates the correlation coefficient and plots a scatter diagram for the *Economics* example given in Table 12.1 in the textbook.

```
Interest_Rate<-c(7.43,7.48,8.00,7.75,7.60,7.63,7.68,7.67,7.59,
                 8.07,8.03,8.00)
Futures_Index<-c(221,222,226,225,224,223,223,226,226,235,233,241)
cor(Interest_Rate,Futures_Index)
```

## [1] 0.8152537

```
plot(Interest_Rate,Futures_Index)
```

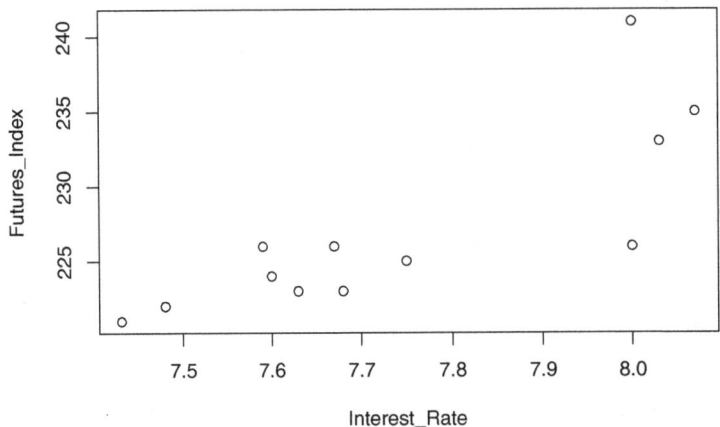

## 12.1 Simple Regression Analysis

The simple regression model establishes a linear relationship between a **dependent variable**, generically denoted by $y$, and an **independent variable**, $x$, as follows:

$$y_i = \beta_0 + \beta_1 x_i + \epsilon_i$$

where

- $x_i$ = value of $x$ for observation $i$
- $y_i$ = value of $y$ for observation $i$
- $\beta_0$ = intercept of the population regression model
- $\beta_1$ = slope of the population regression model
- $\epsilon_i$ = error term for observation $i$

The population parameters $\beta_0$ and $\beta_1$ are unknown; if we estimate them based on a representative sample, we denote the estimates by $b_0$ and $b_1$; we also denote the estimated value of the independent variable for a given value of $x$ by $\hat{y}$, which is calculated using the equation

$$\hat{y}_i = b_0 + b_1 x_i$$

For a particular sample, $b_0$ and $b_1$ are the *sample* intercept and slope.

The R function that calculates a sample regression model is `lm()`, which takes as arguments a `formula` describing the model and the name of the data set. Other

## 12.1. SIMPLE REGRESSION ANALYSIS

R functions, such as coef(), retrieve information from the output created by lm(). The R function summary() synthesizes information from the lm() object and stores it in another object for easier access. As I have mentioned before, the function names(object) shows what information is available in a particular object, an object identified by its name. Here is an example of using the function lm() on the data in *Demonstration Problem 12.1*.

```
beds<-c(23,29,29,35,42,46,50,54,64,66,76,78)
FTEs<-c(69,95,102,118,126,125,138,178,156,184,176,225)
model1<-lm(FTEs~beds)
smodel1<-summary(model1)
names(model1)
```

```
## [1] "coefficients"  "residuals"   "effects"       "rank"
## [5] "fitted.values" "assign"      "qr"            "df.residual"
## [9] "xlevels"       "call"        "terms"         "model"
```

```
names(smodel1)
```

```
## [1] "call"         "terms"       "residuals"    "coefficients"
## [5] "aliased"      "sigma"       "df"           "r.squared"
## [9] "adj.r.squared" "fstatistic" "cov.unscaled"
```

Retrieving a desired piece of information from an object can be done in two ways: either refer to that information by the name of the object followed by the $ sign and the name of the information needed, as in model1$coefficients, or using specialized functions, as in coef(model1). Here is an example in which I retrieve the estimated coefficients $b_0$ and $b_1$ from the smodel1 object.

```
model1$coefficients #This gives the whole list of coefficients
```

```
## (Intercept)       beds
##   30.912470    2.231504
```

```
model1$coefficients[[1]] # This is the first element of the list
```

```
## [1] 30.91247
```

```
model1$coefficients[[2]]
```

```
## [1] 2.231504
```

```
# The same information retrieved otherwise:
b<-coef(model1);b
```

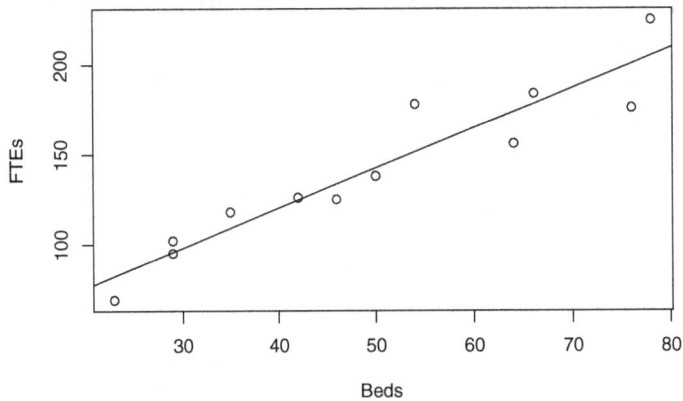

FIGURE 12.1 Scatter plot with regression line

```
## (Intercept)        beds
##    30.912470    2.231504
b0<-coef(model1)[[1]];b0
```

```
## [1] 30.91247
b1<-coef(model1)[[2]];b1
```

```
## [1] 2.231504
# Or by the name of the coefficient:
coef(model1)[["(Intercept)"]]
```

```
## [1] 30.91247
coef(model1)[["beds"]]
```

```
## [1] 2.231504
```

After estimating a model, one can draw the estimated regression line over the scatter diagram, by using the plot function immediately followed by abline(), which, in its simplest form, accepts as an argument the name of a simple linear model. (See the following code lines and the result in Figure 12.1.)

```
plot(FTEs~beds, xlab="Beds")
abline(model1)
```

## 12.2 Residual Analysis

A **residual**, $e_i$, is the difference between an observed value of the dependent variable, $y_i$, and the estimated value of the dependent variable, $\hat{y}_i$, for a given observation $i$.

$$e_i = y_i - \hat{y}_i$$

After running an lm() model, residuals can be retrieved using the function resid(model_name), after which we can plot and examine the residuals. Likewise, we can retrieve the fitted values, $\hat{y}$, using the function fitted(model_name). Here is the *Airline Cost* example.

```
cost<-c(4.28,4.08,4.42,4.17,4.48,4.3,4.82,4.7,5.11,5.13,5.64,5.56)
passengers<-c(61,63,67,69,70,74,76,81,86,91,95,97)
model2<-lm(cost~passengers)
smodel2<-summary(model2)
residuals<-resid(model2)
predicted_y<-fitted(model2)
head(cbind(passengers,cost,predicted_y,residuals),5)
```

```
##   passengers cost predicted_y   residuals
## 1         61 4.28    4.052590  0.22740971
## 2         63 4.08    4.133993 -0.05399349
## 3         67 4.42    4.296800  0.12320012
## 4         69 4.17    4.378203 -0.20820308
## 5         70 4.48    4.418905  0.06109532
```

Figure 12.2 shows a scatter diagram with the regression line and a plot of the residuals in the same example.

```
par(mfrow=c(1,2))
plot(cost~passengers, xlab="Passengers", ylab="Cost")
abline(model2)
plot(residuals~passengers, xlab="Passengers", ylab="Residuals")
abline(h=0,lty=2)
```

*Demonstration Problem 12.2* uses the hospital beds vs. FTEs as above (model1) to show how to diagnose potential problems using various residual plots. The function plot(model_name) produces several regression diagnostic plots, of which the first two are similar to the two in the textbook. (See Figure 12.3.)

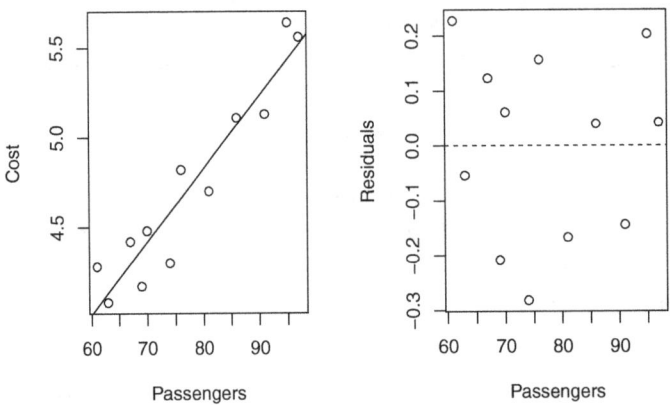

FIGURE 12.2 Regression and Residuals for the Air Cost Example

```
residuals1<-resid(model1)
fitted_FTEs<-fitted(model1)
par(mfrow=c(1,2))
plt1<-plot(model1,which=1:2)
```

We can produce the other two plots as the following code shows. (See the results in Figure 12.4.)

```
par(mfrow=c(1,2))
hist(residuals1, main="", xlab="Residuals 1")
plot(residuals1, type="o",pch=16, ylab="Residuals 1")
```

## 12.3 Standard Error of the Estimate

The standard error of the estimate is given by the formula

$$s_e = \sqrt{\frac{SSE}{n-2}}$$

where $n$ is the number of observations used by the regression model, $n-2$ is the number of degrees of freedom of the model, and $SSE$ is the sum of squared residuals:

$$SSE = \sum (y - \hat{y})^2$$

## 12.3. STANDARD ERROR OF THE ESTIMATE

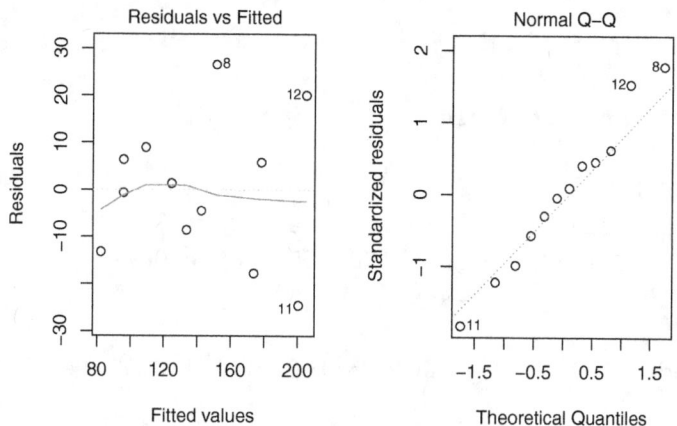

FIGURE 12.3 Regression Plots for the Airline Cost Example

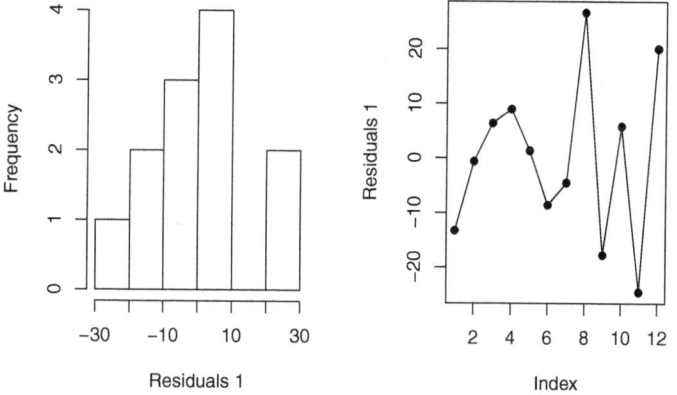

FIGURE 12.4 More Regression Plots for the Airline Cost Example

The function anova() calculates these results after an lm() call; the only argument it requires is the name of the lm() model. Let us use again the hospital beds model to retrieve the standard error of the estimate (see *Demonstration Problem 12.3*).

```
anova(model1) # Produces a number of diagnostic measures

## Analysis of Variance Table
##
## Response: FTEs
##            Df  Sum Sq Mean Sq F value    Pr(>F)
## beds        1 19115.1 19115.1  78.055 4.886e-06 ***
## Residuals  10  2448.9   244.9
## ---
## Signif. codes:  0 '***' 0.001 '**' 0.01 '*' 0.05 '.' 0.1 ' ' 1
```

```
SSE<-anova(model1)[2,2]
cat("SSE =",SSE)

## SSE = 2448.937
```

However, the final value of the standard error of the estimate (which R calls *Residual standard error*) is produced by the lm() function itself and can be retrieved from the summary(model_name) object under the name sigma. In fact, we may denote this standard error by $\hat{\sigma}$, since it is an estimate of $\sigma$, the population standard deviation of the error term $\epsilon$.

```
smodel1

##
## Call:
## lm(formula = FTEs ~ beds)
##
## Residuals:
##      Min       1Q   Median       3Q      Max
## -24.5068  -9.7305   0.3691   7.0267  26.5863
##
## Coefficients:
##             Estimate Std. Error t value Pr(>|t|)
## (Intercept)  30.9125    13.2542   2.332   0.0419 *
```

```
## beds            2.2315     0.2526    8.835 4.89e-06 ***
## ---
## Signif. codes:  0 '***' 0.001 '**' 0.01 '*' 0.05 '.' 0.1 ' ' 1
##
## Residual standard error: 15.65 on 10 degrees of freedom
## Multiple R-squared:  0.8864, Adjusted R-squared:  0.8751
## F-statistic: 78.05 on 1 and 10 DF,  p-value: 4.886e-06
```

Now, we can retrieve $\hat{\sigma}$:

```
sigma_hat<-smodel1$sigma
cat("Residual standard error (standard error of the estimate) =",
    round(sigma_hat),2)
```

```
## Residual standard error (standard error of the estimate) = 16 2
```

## 12.4 Coefficient of Determination

The **coefficient of determination**, $r^2$, measures how well the regression line approximates the observed values of the independent variable. The coefficient of determination is a number between 0 and 1; the closer it is to 1, the better the fit of the model. More precisely, the coefficient of determination gives the share of the variability of the dependent variable (about its mean) that is explained by the independent variable; the remaining share, which is unexplained by the independent variable, is variability in the error term, which includes other factors, not explicitly specified in the regression equation.

The definition of $r^2$ also provides a way of calculating it, as the ratio between the sum of squared deviations of the regression line about the mean of $y$ ($SSR$) and the sum of squared deviations of all $y$ about the mean of $y$ ($SS_{yy}$, or $SST$ as it is denoted in other texts).

$$SS_{yy} = \sum (y - \bar{y})^2$$

$$SSR = \sum (\hat{y} - \bar{y})^2$$

$$SSE = \sum (y - \hat{y})^2$$

$$SS_{yy} = SSR + SSE$$

$$r^2 = \frac{SSR}{SS_{yy}} = 1 - \frac{SSE}{SS_{yy}}$$

The coefficient of determination is given by the R function lm() via its summary(model_name) (see *Demonstration Problem 12.4*).

```
names(smodel1)
```

```
##  [1] "call"          "terms"         "residuals"     "coefficients"
##  [5] "aliased"       "sigma"         "df"            "r.squared"
##  [9] "adj.r.squared" "fstatistic"    "cov.unscaled"
```

```
rsquared<-smodel1$r.squared
cat("    r-squared =",rsquared)
```

```
##     r-squared = 0.886434
```

## 12.5 Hypothesis Tests in a Regression Model

Consider the simple regression model

$$y_i = \beta_0 + \beta_1 x_i + \epsilon_i.$$

Testing the slope is to test the hypothesis that its slope parameter is not significantly different from zero,

$$H_0 : \beta_1 = 0$$
$$H_a : \beta_1 \neq 0$$

A version of the test is a left-tail test

$$H_0 : \beta_1 = 0$$
$$H_a : \beta_1 < 0$$

or a right-tail test,

$$H_0 : \beta_1 = 0$$
$$H_a : \beta_1 > 0$$

For any of these three versions, the test statistic is the $t$-ratio,

$$t = \frac{b_1 - \beta_1}{s_b},$$

## 12.5. HYPOTHESIS TESTS IN A REGRESSION MODEL

where $\beta_1$ is the hypothesized value of the slope and $s_b$ is the sampling standard error of the slope.

R does a two-tail test for all the parameters of the model under the hypothesis,

$$H_0 : \beta_k, \quad H_a \neq 0,$$

which is called a *significance* test. The result of the test is provided in the summary() of the regression object. The following code shows how to retrieve the test results in the airline cost example. (The data and the model are reproduced here for convenience.)

```
cost<-c(4.28,4.08,4.42,4.17,4.48,4.3,4.82,4.7,5.11,5.13,5.64,5.56)
passengers<-c(61,63,67,69,70,74,76,81,86,91,95,97)
model2<-lm(cost~passengers)
smodel2<-summary(model2)
smodel2
```

```
##
## Call:
## lm(formula = cost ~ passengers)
##
## Residuals:
##      Min       1Q   Median       3Q      Max
## -0.28171 -0.14938  0.04101  0.13162  0.22741
##
## Coefficients:
##             Estimate Std. Error t value Pr(>|t|)
## (Intercept) 1.569793   0.338083   4.643 0.000917 ***
## passengers  0.040702   0.004312   9.439 2.69e-06 ***
## ---
## Signif. codes:  0 '***' 0.001 '**' 0.01 '*' 0.05 '.' 0.1 ' ' 1
##
## Residual standard error: 0.1772 on 10 degrees of freedom
## Multiple R-squared:  0.8991, Adjusted R-squared:  0.889
## F-statistic: 89.09 on 1 and 10 DF,  p-value: 2.692e-06
```

Here is how to retrieve the test items from the summary() object.

```
df<-model2$df.residual
se<-coef(smodel2)[2,2]
tratio<-coef(smodel2)[2,3]
pvalue<-coef(smodel2)[2,4]
```

```
cat(" Standard error of slope: se =",se,"\n",
    "t-ratio of slope =",tratio,"\n",
    "p-value of slope =",pvalue,"\n",
    "Ho: slope =0;"," Ha: slope not equal to 0","\n",
    "Reject Ho if p-value < alpha")
```

```
## Standard error of slope: se = 0.004312128
## t-ratio of slope = 9.438865
## p-value of slope = 2.691644e-06
## Ho: slope =0;  Ha: slope not equal to 0
## Reject Ho if p-value < alpha
```

The $p$-value calculated by R covers both tails; therefore, it should be compared to the whole value of a desired significance level, $\alpha$, not only to half of it. To see this, let us calculate the $p$-value explicitly and compare the result to the one produced by R.

```
pvl<-2*(1-pt(abs(tratio),df))
cat("Two-tail p-value calculated explicitely =",pvl)
```

```
## Two-tail p-value calculated explicitely = 2.691644e-06
```

The result is that the (double) $p$-value corresponding to the $t$-ratio calculated above is the same as the one produced by R.

How about a right-tail test? In this case we need to calculate our own $t$-ratio,

$$t = \frac{b_1 - \beta_1}{se(b_1)}.$$

The $p$-value is the area of the right tail of the sampling distribution of $b_1$, limited to the left by the calculated $t$-ratio. Here is an example of such a test (*Demonstration Problem 12.5*, based on the Hospital data); the hypothesis to be tested is

$$H_0 : \beta_1 = 0, \quad H_a : \beta_1 > 0$$

```
# The Hospital data and model, again

beds<-c(23,29,29,35,42,46,50,54,64,66,76,78)
FTEs<-c(69,95,102,118,126,125,138,178,156,184,176,225)
model1<-lm(FTEs~beds)
smodel1<-summary(model1)
df1<-model1$df.residual
t1<-coef(smodel1)[2,3] # Only if the hypothesized beta1 is zero.
```

## 12.5. HYPOTHESIS TESTS IN A REGRESSION MODEL

```
pval1<-1-pt(t1,df1)
cat(" df =",df,"\n","t-ratio =",t1, "\n","p-value =",pval1,"\n",
    "Ho: beta1 = 0,  Ha: beta1 > 0.  Reject Ho if p-value < alpha")
```

```
##  df = 10
##  t-ratio = 8.834848
##  p-value = 2.443154e-06
##  Ho: beta1 = 0,  Ha: beta1 > 0.  Reject Ho if p-value < alpha
```

A left-tail test is similar, but the area is the one to the left of the calculated $t$-ratio. Let us use the same hospital data, but test the following hypothesis:

$$H_0 : \beta_1 = 3, \; H_a : \beta_1 < 3$$

The differences with respect to the solution to *Demonstration Problem 12.5* are

- the way we produce the $t$-ratio (we need to calculate it, because the hypothesized $\beta_1$ is not zero anymore),
- the fact that we need to retrieve $b_1$ and $s_b$, and
- how we calculate the $p$-value.

```
beds<-c(23,29,29,35,42,46,50,54,64,66,76,78)
FTEs<-c(69,95,102,118,126,125,138,178,156,184,176,225)
beta1<-3
model1<-lm(FTEs~beds)
smodel1<-summary(model1)
b1<-coef(smodel1)[2,1]
seb1<-coef(smodel1)[2,2]
df1<-model1$df.residual
t1<-(b1-beta1)/seb1 # Only if the hypothesized beta1 is zero
pval1<-pt(t1,df1)
cat("    Ho: beta1 =",beta1,";   Ha: beta1 <",beta1,"\n",
    "   b1 =",b1,"\n",
    "   se(b1) =",seb1,"\n",
    "   df =",df,"\n",
    "   t-ratio =",t1, "\n",
    "   p-value =",pval1,"\n",
    "   Reject Ho if p-value < alpha")
```

```
##     Ho: beta1 = 3 ;  Ha: beta1 < 3
##     b1 = 2.231504
##     se(b1) = 0.2525798
```

```
##     df = 10
##     t-ratio = -3.042587
##     p-value = 0.006203836
##     Reject Ho if p-value < alpha
```

The test for the overall significance of the model is an $F$-test with the null hypothesis that all the slope parameters are simultaneously zero. Since we only have one slope parameter in the simple regression model, the overall significance test produces the same result as the $t$-test for the significance of the slope parameter. The following example uses the airplane cost data to show how to retrieve the $F$-statistic and the corresponding $p$-value from the regression output.

```
# The airplane cost data and model, again:
cost<-c(4.28,4.08,4.42,4.17,4.48,4.3,4.82,4.7,5.11,5.13,5.64,5.56)
passengers<-c(61,63,67,69,70,74,76,81,86,91,95,97)
model2<-lm(cost~passengers)
amodel2<-anova(model2)
amodel2
```

```
## Analysis of Variance Table
##
## Response: cost
##              Df  Sum Sq Mean Sq F value    Pr(>F)
## passengers    1 2.79803 2.79803  89.092 2.692e-06 ***
## Residuals    10 0.31406 0.03141
## ---
## Signif. codes:  0 '***' 0.001 '**' 0.01 '*' 0.05 '.' 0.1 ' ' 1
```

The function producing the information necessary to compute the $F$-statistic, and also producing the $F$-statistic itself and its $p$-value is anova(), which we have already applied in the above code lines; the next code lines just retrieve the results from the anova() object.

```
fstat<-amodel2[1,4]
fpval<-amodel2[1,5]
cat("   Ho: All slopes are equal to zero","\n",
    "  Ha: At least one slope is not zero","\n",
    "  F =",fstat,"\n",
    "  p-value =",fpval)
```

```
##     Ho: All slopes are equal to zero
```

## 12.6. ESTIMATION

```
##      Ha: At least one slope is not zero
##      F = 89.09218
##      p-value = 2.691644e-06
```

## 12.6 Estimation

A regression model can be used, besides inferences about the slope, to estimate (predict) the expected value of the dependent variable for a given level of the independent variable. This estimate will be a random variable since it is determined using the estimates of the regression coefficients, which are also random variables. Therefore, the predicted value of $y$, $\hat{y}$, has a sampling distribution and can generate a confidence interval. Similarly, one can use the same regression model to predict a particular value of $y$, not only its expectation; in this case the confidence interval will be larger, while the point estimate is the same as the predicted average.

The R function predict(model_name) predicts both the average $y$ and a particular value of $y$; the distinction is made by the parameter interval. When interval is equal to "confidence," we get a prediction of the average $y$; when it is equal to "prediction," we get a prediction about a particular value.

The predict() function requires that the value(s) of $x$ for which the prediction is made be organized as a data.frame. The syntax of the predict() function can be found in the predict.lm() help information.

Let us calculate these predictions and their confidence intervals for *Demonstration Problem 12.6*, which is, again, based on the hospital data.

```
beds<-c(23,29,29,35,42,46,50,54,64,66,76,78)
FTEs<-c(69,95,102,118,126,125,138,178,156,184,176,225)
cl<-0.95
x<-40
newd<-data.frame(beds=x)
model1<-lm(FTEs~beds)
pred<-predict(model1,newdata=newd,interval="confidence",level=cl)
cat("   Confidence Interval for Average FTEs:","\n",
    "   Number of beds =",x,"\n",
    "   Fitted value =",pred[1],"\n",
    "   Lower bound =",pred[2],"\n",
    "   Upper bound =",pred[3])
```

```
##      Confidence Interval for Average FTEs:
```

```
##    Number of beds = 40
##    Fitted value = 120.1726
##    Lower bound = 108.8189
##    Upper bound = 131.5263
```

Now, let us predict a confidence interval for a particular value of the dependent variable.

```
pred1<-predict(model1,newdata=newd,interval="prediction",level=cl)
cat("   Confidence Interval for a particular FTE:","\n",
    "  Number of beds =",x,"\n",
    "  Fitted value =",pred1[1],"\n",
    "  Lower bound =",pred1[2],"\n",
    "  Upper bound =",pred1[3])
```

```
##    Confidence Interval for a particular FTE:
##    Number of beds = 40
##    Fitted value = 120.1726
##    Lower bound = 83.50239
##    Upper bound = 156.8429
```

Next, we would like to visualize these confidence intervals for all observations in a compact graph. To this purpose, I am going to create an artificial array of the beds variable, then use our estimated model to calculate predictions for all these artificial data. Figure 12.5 shows the results.

```
newx<-data.frame(beds=22:80)
cnf<-predict(model1,newdata=newx,interval="confidence",level=cl)
prd<-predict(model1,newdata=newx,interval="prediction",level=cl)
matplot(newx, cbind(cnf[,1], cnf[,2], cnf[,3],prd[,2], prd[,3]),
    type ="l", lty=c(1, 2, 2, 3, 3),
    col=c("black", "red", "red", "blue", "blue"),
    ylab="FTEs", xlab="Number of Beds")
points(beds, FTEs)
legend("topleft",
legend=c("E[y|x]", "lwr_CI", "upr_CI",
"lwr_PI","upr_PI"),
lty=c(1, 2, 2, 3, 3),
col=c("black", "red", "red", "blue", "blue"))
```

## 12.7. FORECASTING TREND LINE

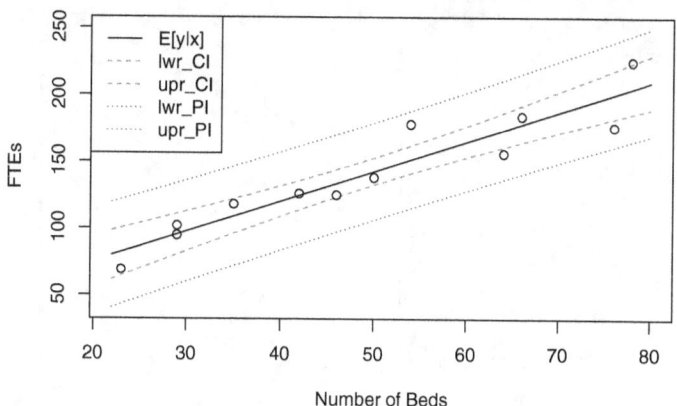

FIGURE 12.5 Confidence Bands for Prediction in the Hospital Example

## 12.7 Forecasting Trend Line

The R function `ts()` creates time series data out of a vector, matrix, or data frame. Its main arguments are

- data set name
- frequency (number of observation per period, for example, frequency is 7 for daily data when the period is a week, or 12 for monthly data when the period is a year)
- the start period, for instance `start=2007` for yearly data, or `start=c(2007,5)` for monthly data. The next code fragment plots sales over a period of 10 years, from 2007 to 2016 (data from Table 12.8 in the textbook), as well as a trend line. Figure 12.6 shows these graphs.

```
sales<-c(7.84,12.26,13.11,15.78,21.29,25.68,23.8,26.43,29.16,33.06)
time<-2007:2016
m1<-lm(sales~time)
b0<-coef(m1)[[1]]
b1<-coef(m1)[[2]]
par(mfrow=c(1,2))
plot(time,sales,ylab="Sales (in millions)",xlab="Year")
plot(time,sales,ylab="Sales (in millions)",xlab="Year")
abline(b0,b1)
```

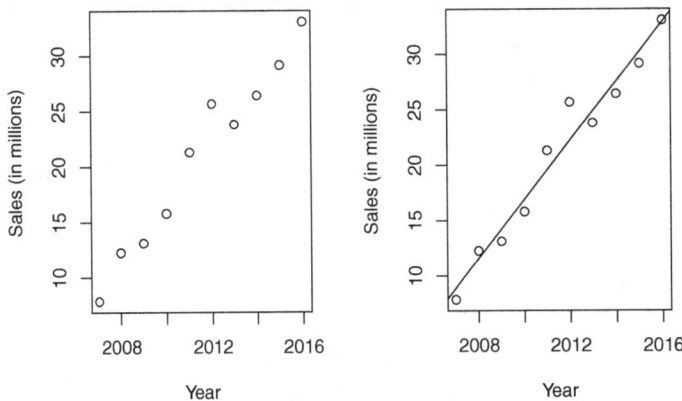

FIGURE 12.6 Time Series Plots for the Sales Data

We can now forecast sales in year 2019 using the trend equation that we have just determined.

```
yhat2019<-b0+b1*2019
yhat2019
```

```
## [1] 40.856
```

## 12.8 Interpreting the Output

Let us use the airline cost data as an example to identify the main items in regression output. I reproduce here the data, for convenience. Most of the results of a regression computation can be found in the summary(model_name) and anova(model_name) objects. We have already seen how to extract various information items from these objects.

```
cost<-c(4.28,4.08,4.42,4.17,4.48,4.3,4.82,4.7,5.11,5.13,5.64,5.56)
passengers<-c(61,63,67,69,70,74,76,81,86,91,95,97)
model2<-lm(cost~passengers)
smodel2<-summary(model2)
amodel2<-anova(model2)
```

## 12.8. INTERPRETING THE OUTPUT

The summary of the model shows the formula, some summary statistics of the residuals, the coefficients with their standard errors, $t$-values, $p$-values, the residual standard error ($\hat{\sigma}$), $r^2$, the test for overall significance of the regression, and the $F$-statistic with its $p$-value.

```
smodel2 # This is a summary output of model2 #

##
## Call:
## lm(formula = cost ~ passengers)
##
## Residuals:
##      Min      1Q   Median      3Q     Max
## -0.28171 -0.14938  0.04101  0.13162  0.22741
##
## Coefficients:
##             Estimate Std. Error t value Pr(>|t|)
## (Intercept) 1.569793   0.338083   4.643 0.000917 ***
## passengers  0.040702   0.004312   9.439 2.69e-06 ***
## ---
## Signif. codes:  0 '***' 0.001 '**' 0.01 '*' 0.05 '.' 0.1 ' ' 1
##
## Residual standard error: 0.1772 on 10 degrees of freedom
## Multiple R-squared:  0.8991, Adjusted R-squared:  0.889
## F-statistic: 89.09 on 1 and 10 DF,  p-value: 2.692e-06
```

The anova() object contains mainly the various sum of squares and mean squares generated by the model.

```
amodel2 #   This is output generated by the anova() function   #

## Analysis of Variance Table
##
## Response: cost
##            Df Sum Sq Mean Sq F value    Pr(>F)
## passengers  1 2.79803 2.79803  89.092 2.692e-06 ***
## Residuals  10 0.31406 0.03141
## ---
## Signif. codes:  0 '***' 0.001 '**' 0.01 '*' 0.05 '.' 0.1 ' ' 1
```

# Chapter 13

# Multiple Regression Analysis

The multiple regression model is similar to the simple model we have studied in Chapter 12, but includes more than one dependent variable. This apparently minor difference has important consequences, from interpreting the regression coefficients to new possibilities of creative functional forms of the model. The general form of the multiple regression model is the following:

$$y = \beta_0 + \beta_1 x_1 + \beta_2 x_2 + ... + \beta_k x_k + \epsilon$$

The slope coefficient $\beta_i$ represents the change in $y$ when $x_i$ increases by one unit while all the other independent variables remain constant. In R, a multiple regression model is technically no different from a simple one; the same function `lm()` estimates the model, and the same other functions help visualizing the data and the results or provide various information items after estimating ("fitting") a model. Here is the example in Table 13.1 of the textbook.

```
# Real Estate Data (price in $1000s):
price<-c(63.0,65.1,69.9,76.8,73.9,77.9,74.9,78.0,79.0,83.4,79.5,83.9,
    79.7,84.5,96.0,109.5,102.5,121.0,104.9,128.0,129.0,117.9,140.0)
sqfeet<-c(1605,2489,1553,2404,1884,1558,1748,3105,1682,2470,1820,2143,
    2121,2485,2300,2714,2463,3076,3048,3267,3069,4765,4540)
age<-c(35,45,20,32,25,14,8,10,28,30,2,6,14,9,19,4,5,7,3,6,10,11,8)
realest<-data.frame(price,sqfeet,age)
```

Here is the head of the real estate data frame.

`head(realest)`

```
##   price sqfeet age
```

```
## 1   63.0   1605   35
## 2   65.1   2489   45
## 3   69.9   1553   20
## 4   76.8   2404   32
## 5   73.9   1884   25
## 6   77.9   1558   14
```

The following table gives the summary statistics data set:

```
summary(realest)
```

```
##      price            sqfeet          age
##  Min.   : 63.00   Min.   :1553   Min.   : 2.00
##  1st Qu.: 77.35   1st Qu.:1852   1st Qu.: 6.50
##  Median : 83.40   Median :2463   Median :10.00
##  Mean   : 92.10   Mean   :2535   Mean   :15.26
##  3rd Qu.:107.20   3rd Qu.:3058   3rd Qu.:22.50
##  Max.   :140.00   Max.   :4765   Max.   :45.00
```

Finally, Figure 13.1 shows all pair-wise scatter diagrams related to the real estate data. In a multiple regression model, though, such pair-wise plots are not very informative, since each point, which represents a complete observation, is determined by different values of all independent variables. Partial effects, on the other hand, require that the other variables in the model stay constant when assessing the effect of one variable on $y$, the dependent variable. Let us now draw the $3 \times 3$ matrix of pair-wise scatter plots.

```
plot(realest)
```

The next code lines regress price on the surface area of a house and its age and show a summary of the output, as well as the anova() table.

```
mod1<-lm(price~sqfeet+age,data=realest)
summary(mod1)
```

```
##
## Call:
## lm(formula = price ~ sqfeet + age, data = realest)
##
## Residuals:
##      Min       1Q   Median       3Q      Max
## -27.7018  -6.8938  -0.1728   7.1340  23.9361
```

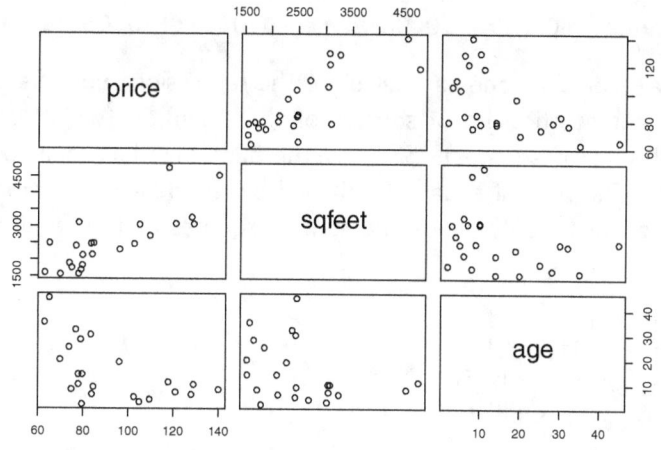

FIGURE 13.1 Pair-wise Plots for the Real Estate Data

```
## 
## Coefficients:
##              Estimate Std. Error t value Pr(>|t|)
## (Intercept) 57.350746  10.007152   5.731 1.31e-05 ***
## sqfeet       0.017718   0.003146   5.633 1.64e-05 ***
## age         -0.666348   0.227997  -2.923  0.00842 **
## ---
## Signif. codes:  0 '***' 0.001 '**' 0.01 '*' 0.05 '.' 0.1 ' ' 1
## 
## Residual standard error: 11.96 on 20 degrees of freedom
## Multiple R-squared:  0.7411, Adjusted R-squared:  0.7152
## F-statistic: 28.63 on 2 and 20 DF,  p-value: 1.353e-06
```

```
anova(mod1)
```

```
## Analysis of Variance Table
## 
## Response: price
##           Df Sum Sq Mean Sq F value    Pr(>F)
## sqfeet     1 6967.8  6967.8 48.7087 8.976e-07 ***
## age        1 1221.9  1221.9  8.5417  0.008418 **
## Residuals 20 2861.0   143.1
```

```
## ---
## Signif. codes:   0 '***' 0.001 '**' 0.01 '*' 0.05 '.' 0.1 ' ' 1
```

From the anova() output, one can calculate the regression sum of squares, which we have previously named the sum of squares of the estimate, (which is also sometimes called the total sum of squares), SSE, as the sum of all lines in column 2 of the anova() object. The sum of squares explained by the dependent variables altogether, SSreg is, then, equal to SSE minus the sum of squares of the residuals, which I will refer to here as SSerr:

```
SSE<-sum(anova(mod1)[,2])
SSerr<-anova(mod1)[3,2]
SSreg<-SSE-SSerr
cat("    SSE =",SSE,"\n","   SSerr =",SSerr,"\n","   SSreg =",SSreg)
```

```
##    SSE = 11050.74
##    SSerr = 2861.017
##    SSreg = 8189.723
```

Once we have the results of the regression model, we can calculate, for example, an estimate of the price for a house having the surface area equal to 2500 square feet and being 12 years old. As a bonus, the predict() function gives us a 95% confidence interval for that estimate.

```
newdata<-data.frame(sqfeet=2500,age=12)
yhat<-predict(mod1,newdata=newdata,interval="confidence")
cat("   y_hat =",yhat[[1]],"\n",
    "  lowCI =",yhat[[2]],"\n",
    "  uppCI =",yhat[[3]])
```

```
##    y_hat = 93.64966
##    lowCI = 88.19471
##    uppCI = 99.10461
```

Our next task is to reproduce the example in *Demonstration Problem 13.1*, which I will refer to as the interest rate problem.

```
year<-c(1986,1988,1990,1992,1994,1996,1998,2000,2002,2004,
        2006,2008,2010,2012,2014)
prime<-c(8.33,9.32,10.01,6.25,7.15,8.27,8.35,9.23,4.67,4.34,
        7.96,5.09,3.25,3.25,3.25)
```

```
unempl<-c(7.0,5.5,5.6,7.5,6.1,5.4,4.5,4.0,5.8,5.5,4.6,5.8,9.6,8.1,6.2)
saving<-c(8.2,7.3,7.0,7.7,4.8,4.0,4.3,2.3,2.4,2.1,0.7,1.8,5.8,7.6,4.8)
interest<-data.frame(year,prime,unempl,saving)
head(interest)
```

```
##   year prime unempl saving
## 1 1986  8.33    7.0    8.2
## 2 1988  9.32    5.5    7.3
## 3 1990 10.01    5.6    7.0
## 4 1992  6.25    7.5    7.7
## 5 1994  7.15    6.1    4.8
## 6 1996  8.27    5.4    4.0
```

Creating a data frame from the data, as I have done above, is not necessary for our immediate purpose, but sometimes it is easier to handle the data that way.

Next, we regress the prime interest rate on the other two independent variables, the unemployment rate and the personal saving, and examine the results. Extracting specific information from the summary() and anova() objects can be done the same way as for the simple regression model.

```
mod2<-lm(prime~unempl+saving, data=interest)
summary(mod2)
```

```
## 
## Call:
## lm(formula = prime ~ unempl + saving, data = interest)
## 
## Residuals:
##     Min      1Q  Median      3Q     Max
## -3.1846 -0.7148  0.0754  1.0092  1.8082
## 
## Coefficients:
##             Estimate Std. Error t value Pr(>|t|)
## (Intercept)  13.5786     1.7276   7.860 4.5e-06 ***
## unempl       -1.6622     0.3372  -4.929 0.000349 ***
## saving        0.6586     0.1990   3.309 0.006234 **
## ---
## Signif. codes:  0 '***' 0.001 '**' 0.01 '*' 0.05 '.' 0.1 ' ' 1
## 
## Residual standard error: 1.496 on 12 degrees of freedom
```

```
## Multiple R-squared:  0.6719, Adjusted R-squared:  0.6172
## F-statistic: 12.29 on 2 and 12 DF,  p-value: 0.001248
```
```
anova(mod2)
```
```
## Analysis of Variance Table
## 
## Response: prime
##           Df Sum Sq Mean Sq F value   Pr(>F)
## unempl     1 30.478 30.4781  13.620 0.003089 **
## saving     1 24.505 24.5054  10.951 0.006234 **
## Residuals 12 26.854  2.2378
## ---
## Signif. codes:  0 '***' 0.001 '**' 0.01 '*' 0.05 '.' 0.1 ' ' 1
```

## 13.1 Significance Tests in Multiple Regression

Testing the overall model is to test that all the slope coefficients are simultaneously equal to zero against the alternative that at least one is different from zero.

$$H_0 : \beta_1 = \beta_2 = ... = \beta_k = 0$$

$H_a$ : At least one of the slope coefficients is not zero

The $F$-statistic tests the overall significance of the model and it is given by the formula

$$F = \frac{MS_{reg}}{MS_{err}} = \frac{SS_{reg}/df_{reg}}{SS_{err}/df_{err}} = \frac{SSR/k}{SSE/(N-k-1)}.$$

The following example reproduces the real estate model and its summary.

```
mod1<-lm(price~sqfeet+age,data=realest)
smod1<-summary(mod1)
smod1
```
```
## 
## Call:
## lm(formula = price ~ sqfeet + age, data = realest)
## 
## Residuals:
##      Min      1Q  Median      3Q     Max
## -27.7018 -6.8938 -0.1728  7.1340 23.9361
```

## 13.1. SIGNIFICANCE TESTS IN MULTIPLE REGRESSION

```
## 
## Coefficients:
##              Estimate Std. Error t value Pr(>|t|)
## (Intercept) 57.350746  10.007152   5.731 1.31e-05 ***
## sqfeet       0.017718   0.003146   5.633 1.64e-05 ***
## age         -0.666348   0.227997  -2.923 0.00842  **
## ---
## Signif. codes:  0 '***' 0.001 '**' 0.01 '*' 0.05 '.' 0.1 ' ' 1
## 
## Residual standard error: 11.96 on 20 degrees of freedom
## Multiple R-squared:  0.7411, Adjusted R-squared:  0.7152
## F-statistic: 28.63 on 2 and 20 DF,  p-value: 1.353e-06
```

To retrieve the values of the $F$-statistic and its degrees of freedom, we need to access the three elements of the vector model_name$fstatistic, but we need to calculate the $p$-value, since it is not saved by the lm() function.

```
fstat<-smod1$fstatistic[[1]]
df_numerator<-smod1$fstatistic[[2]]
df_denominator<-smod1$fstatistic[[3]]
pval<-1-pf(fstat,df_numerator,df_denominator)
cat(" F-statistic =",smod1$fstatistic[[1]],"\n",
    "df_regression =",smod1$fstatistic[[2]],"\n",
    "df_errors =",smod1$fstatistic[[3]],"\n",
    "p-value of F-test =",pval)
```

```
##  F-statistic = 28.62522
##  df_regression = 2
##  df_errors = 20
##  p-value of F-test = 1.352978e-06
```

The regression summary output contains the $p$-values of the coefficients of the regression model in the coefficients table, from where we can extract the $t$-statistics and the $p$-values as shown in the next code fragment.

```
t_sqfeet<-coefficients(smod1)[2,3]
t_age<-coefficients(smod1)[3,3]
pv_sqfeet<-coefficients(smod1)[2,4]
pv_age<-coefficients(smod1)[3,4]
cat(" t-ratio for sqfeet =",t_sqfeet,"\n",
```

```
      "t-ratio for age =",t_age,"\n",
      "p-value for sqfeet =",pv_sqfeet,"\n",
      "p-value for age =",pv_age)
```

```
## t-ratio for sqfeet = 5.632605
## t-ratio for age = -2.922621
## p-value for sqfeet = 1.635354e-05
## p-value for age = 0.008417613
```

An example of opening a data file for a textbook problem and solving the problem is given below. The problem in question is Problem 13.11, which requires regressing $y$ on the other variables in the data set. We first load the data set, then display the head of the table to see the variable names, and finally we run the regression and show its summary output. Please make sure you use capital letters for the variables, as they are shown in the data file (the textbook uses lower case letters).

```
library(Black9edata)
data(p13.11)
head(p13.11)
```

```
## # A tibble: 6 x 4
##        Y    X1    X2    X3
##    <dbl> <dbl> <dbl> <dbl>
## 1   5.30  44.0  11.0   401
## 2   3.60  24.0  40.0   219
## 3   5.10  46.0  13.0   394
## 4   4.90  38.0  18.0   362
## 5   7.00  61.0   3.00  453
## 6   6.40  58.0   5.00  468
```

```
mod13.11<-lm(Y~X1+X2+X3,data=p13.11)
summary(mod13.11)
```

```
## 
## Call:
## lm(formula = Y ~ X1 + X2 + X3, data = p13.11)
## 
## Residuals:
##      Min       1Q   Median       3Q      Max
## -0.29743 -0.16546  0.00938  0.14973  0.41039
## 
```

```
## Coefficients:
##              Estimate Std. Error t value Pr(>|t|)
## (Intercept)  3.980769   1.573044   2.531  0.02794 *
## X1           0.073216   0.020890   3.505  0.00493 **
## X2          -0.032322   0.020896  -1.547  0.15018
## X3          -0.003886   0.003833  -1.014  0.33248
## ---
## Signif. codes:  0 '***' 0.001 '**' 0.01 '*' 0.05 '.' 0.1 ' ' 1
##
## Residual standard error: 0.2331 on 11 degrees of freedom
## Multiple R-squared:  0.9648, Adjusted R-squared:  0.9552
## F-statistic: 100.5 on 3 and 11 DF,  p-value: 2.822e-08
```

## 13.2 Residuals, Stdandard Error of Estimate, and R-Squared

As for the simple regression model, the multiple regression model produces residuals for all the observations in the data set, which can be retrieved from the regression output with the function resid(). The following example uses the realest data frame, which contains the date for the real estate example (the textbook uses rounded values when computing the residuals, hence the slight differences.)

```
mod1<-lm(price~sqfeet+age,data=realest)
head(realest)
```

```
##   price sqfeet age
## 1  63.0   1605  35
## 2  65.1   2489  45
## 3  69.9   1553  20
## 4  76.8   2404  32
## 5  73.9   1884  25
## 6  77.9   1558  14
```

```
yhat<-57.4+.0177*realest$sqfeet-.666*realest$age
restext<-realest$price-yhat
rmod1<-resid(mod1)
dfr<-data.frame(realest$price,round(restext,4),round(rmod1,3))
names(dfr)<-c("price","approximate residuals","precise residuals")
head(dfr)
```

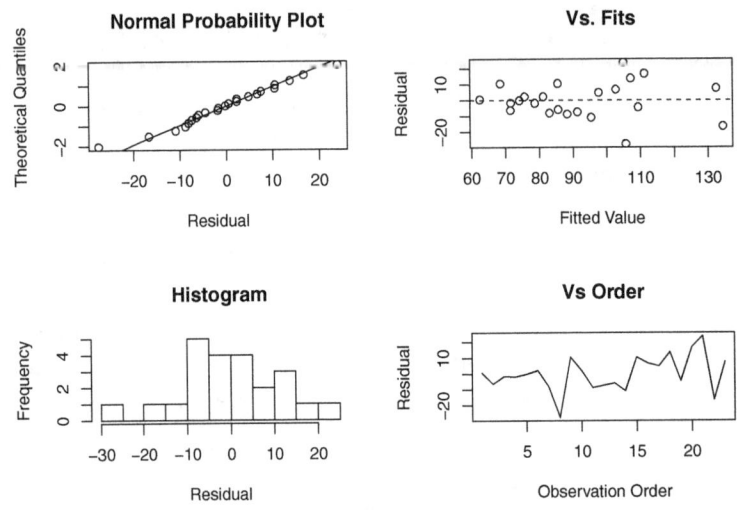

FIGURE 13.2 Real Estate Regression Results

```
##   price approximate residuals precise residuals
## 1  63.0               0.5015             0.534
## 2  65.1              -6.3853            -6.365
## 3  69.9              -1.6681            -1.640
## 4  76.8              -1.8388            -1.822
## 5  73.9              -0.1968            -0.173
## 6  77.9               2.2474             2.273
```

Figure 13.2 shows four plots of various regression results.

```
par(mfrow=c(2,2))#Allows plotting a 2 by 2 matrix of graphs
qqnorm(rmod1,datax=TRUE,main="Normal Probability Plot",
    ylab="Residual")
qqline(rmod1,datax=TRUE)
plot(fitted(mod1),rmod1,main="Vs. Fits",xlab="Fitted Value",
    ylab="Residual")
abline(h=0,lty=2)
hist(rmod1,freq=TRUE,breaks=10,ylab="Frequency",xlab="Residual",
    main="Histogram")
plot(rmod1,type="l",main="Vs Order",xlab="Observation Order",
    ylab="Residual")
```

How can one retrieve the sum of squared errors ($SSE$) from the output of a multiple

## 13.2. RESIDUALS, STDANDARD ERROR OF ESTIMATE, AND R-SQUARED

regression model? As before, the various sum of square values are computed by the function anova(), which takes as its main argument the name of a model previously estimated. Let us retrieve the $SSE$ and the various degrees of freedom from the real estate model and calculate the standard error of the estimate; in the following formula, $s_e$ is the standard error of the estimate, $n$ is the number of observations used by the model, and $k$ is the number of $\beta$ parameters to be estimated.

$$s_e = \sqrt{\frac{SSE}{n-k-1}}$$

```
mod1<-lm(price~sqfeet+age,data=realest)
amod1<-anova(mod1)
SSE<-amod1[3,2]
dfres<-df.residual(mod1)
s<-sqrt(SSE/dfres)
cat("   SSE =",SSE,"\n",
    " DF residuals =",dfres,"\n",
    " Standard error of esitmate, s =",s)
```

```
##    SSE = 2861.017
##  DF residuals = 20
##  Standard error of esitmate, s = 11.96039
```

R produces the standard error of estimate, which can be retrieved from the summary() object, as follows:

```
smod1<-summary(mod1)
sig<-smod1$sigma
cat(" Standard error of regression produced py R, s =",sig)
```

```
##  Standard error of regression produced py R, s = 11.96039
```

A normal distribution of the residuals would have its mean 0, about 68% of the residuals would be between $-s_e$ and $s_e$, and about 95% of them would be between $-2s_e$ and $2s_e$. Let us calculate these percentages for the real estate model. The next code lines show how to select elements out of a vector based on criteria. The function length() returns the total number of elements in a vector.

```
res<-resid(mod1)
resid2s<-res[res>=-s & res<=s]
resid4s<-res[res>=-2*s & res<=2*s]
```

```
p2s<-length(resid2s)/nobs(mod1)*100
p4s<-length(resid4s)/nobs(mod1)*100
cat(" Two st.dev. span: theoretical = 68 percent, residuals =",
    round(p2s,0),"percent","\n",
    "Four st.dev. span: theoretical = 95 percent, residuals =",
    round(p4s,0),"percent")
```

```
##  Two st.dev. span: theoretical = 68 percent, residuals = 78 percent
##  Four st.dev. span: theoretical = 95 percent, residuals = 91 percent
```

The **coefficient of multiple determination**, $R^2$, gives us a measure of the goodness of fit of the multiple regression model. It can be calculated with the formula

$$R^2 = \frac{SSR}{SS_{yy}} = 1 - \frac{SSE}{SS_{yy}}$$

An inconvenience of $R^2$ is that it increases with any new factor introduced in the regression model; an alternative measure of goodness of fit, the adjusted $R^2$, tries to remedy this inconvenience. The adjusted $R^2$ formula is

$$\text{Adjusted } R^2 = 1 - \frac{SSE/(n-k-1)}{SS_{yy}/(n-1)}.$$

All the items that are necessary to calculate $R^2$ and adjusted $R^2$ can be retrieved from the anova() output.

```
mod1<-lm(price~sqfeet+age,data=realest)
smod1<-summary(mod1)
amod1<-anova(mod1)
SSE<-amod1[3,2] #Residual sum of squares
SSyy<-sum(amod1[,2]) #total sum of squares
nk1<-df.residual(mod1)
n1<-nobs(mod1)-1
Rsq<-1-SSE/SSyy
AdjRsq<-1-(SSE/nk1)/(SSyy/n1)
cat(" R-squared =",Rsq,"\n","Adjusted R-squared =",AdjRsq)
```

```
##  R-squared = 0.7411018
##  Adjusted R-squared = 0.715212
```

## 13.3 Interpreting Regression Output

The main sources for regression results are the objects created by the functions lm(), summary(), and anova(). The summary() function is, perhaps, the best place to find the coefficients of the regression, their standard errors, $t$-ratios, and $p$-values. It also provides the standard error of the estimate, $s_e$, which it calls the "Residual standard error," $R^2$, adjusted $R^2$, and the overall significance of the regression, the $F$-statistic with its $p$-value.

The function anova() is the place to go when we are interested in the various sums of squares, mean squares, and degrees of freedom.

*Demonstration Problem 13.2*

```
year<-c(1986,1988,1990,1992,1994,1996,1998,2000,2002,2004,2006,
        2008,2010,2012,2014)
prime<-c(8.33,9.32,10.01,6.25,7.15,8.27,8.35,9.23,4.67,4.34,7.96,
        5.09,3.25,3.25,3.25)
unempl<-c(7.0,5.5,5.6,7.5,6.1,5.4,4.5,4.0,5.8,5.5,4.6,5.8,9.6,8.1,6.2)
saving<-c(8.2,7.3,7.0,7.7,4.8,4.0,4.3,2.3,2.4,2.1,0.7,1.8,5.8,7.6,4.8)
interest<-data.frame(year,prime,unempl,saving)
mod2<-lm(prime~unempl+saving, data=interest)
summary(mod2)
```

```
##
## Call:
## lm(formula = prime ~ unempl + saving, data = interest)
##
## Residuals:
##     Min      1Q  Median      3Q     Max
## -3.1846 -0.7148  0.0754  1.0092  1.8082
##
## Coefficients:
##             Estimate Std. Error t value Pr(>|t|)
## (Intercept)  13.5786     1.7276   7.860 4.5e-06 ***
## unempl       -1.6622     0.3372  -4.929 0.000349 ***
## saving        0.6586     0.1990   3.309 0.006234 **
## ---
## Signif. codes:  0 '***' 0.001 '**' 0.01 '*' 0.05 '.' 0.1 ' ' 1
##
## Residual standard error: 1.496 on 12 degrees of freedom
```

```
## Multiple R-squared:  0.6719, Adjusted R-squared:  0.6172
## F-statistic: 12.29 on 2 and 12 DF,  p-value: 0.001248
```
```
anova(mod2)
```
```
## Analysis of Variance Table
## 
## Response: prime
##           Df Sum Sq Mean Sq F value   Pr(>F)
## unempl     1 30.478 30.4781  13.620 0.003089 **
## saving     1 24.505 24.5054  10.951 0.006234 **
## Residuals 12 26.854  2.2378
## ---
## Signif. codes:  0 '***' 0.001 '**' 0.01 '*' 0.05 '.' 0.1 ' ' 1
```

# Chapter 14

# Building Regression Models

## 14.1 Nonlinear Models

A **quadratic** model is one in which some of the variables appear both as linear and quadratic (i.e., squared) terms, as the following generic example shows:

$$y = \beta_0 + \beta_1 x_1 + \beta_2 x_1^2 + \epsilon$$

In R, one can include a quadratic term like $x_1^2$ directly in a regression model by writing it as I(x1^2), or can previously create a new variable such as $z = x_1^2$. Here is an example based on the data in Table 14.1, the manufacturing data.

```
sales<-c(2.1,3.6,6.2,10.4,22.8,35.6,57.12,83.5,109.4,128.6,196.8,
         280.0,462.3) # sales, in millions
reps<-c(2,1,2,3,4,4,5,5,6,7,8,10,11) # number of representatives
lin<-lm(sales~reps) # linear model
slin<-summary(lin)
alin<-anova(lin)
slin;alin

##
## Call:
## lm(formula = sales ~ reps)
##
## Residuals:
##     Min      1Q  Median      3Q     Max
## -51.55  -29.73  -21.48   27.07  118.04
```

```
## 
## Coefficients:
##              Estimate Std. Error t value Pr(>|t|)
## (Intercept) -107.027     28.737  -3.724  0.00336 **
## reps          41.026      4.779   8.584 3.32e-06 ***
## ---
## Signif. codes:  0 '***' 0.001 '**' 0.01 '*' 0.05 '.' 0.1 ' ' 1
## 
## Residual standard error: 51.1 on 11 degrees of freedom
## Multiple R-squared:  0.8701, Adjusted R-squared:  0.8583
## F-statistic: 73.69 on 1 and 11 DF,  p-value: 3.321e-06

## Analysis of Variance Table
## 
## Response: sales
##           Df Sum Sq Mean Sq F value    Pr(>F)
## reps       1 192395  192395  73.689 3.321e-06 ***
## Residuals 11  28720    2611
## ---
## Signif. codes:  0 '***' 0.001 '**' 0.01 '*' 0.05 '.' 0.1 ' ' 1
```

Let us compare the two scatter plots shown in Figure 14.1: one shows *sales* against *reps*, and the other shows *sales* against $reps^2$. The following code sequence builds these scatter plots:

```
par(mfrow=c(1,2))
plot(reps,sales, xlab="Reps", ylab="Sales")
plot(reps^2,sales, xlab="Squared Reps", ylab="Sales")
```

Comparing the two plots suggests that the *sales* vs. $reps^2$ graph is closer to a straight line; therefore, a linear regression model with $reps^2$ is more appropriate.

Here is the quadratic (second-order) regression model for the manufacturing data.

```
qdr<-lm(sales~reps+I(reps^2))
summary(qdr)
```

```
## 
## Call:
## lm(formula = sales ~ reps + I(reps^2))
```

## 14.1. NONLINEAR MODELS

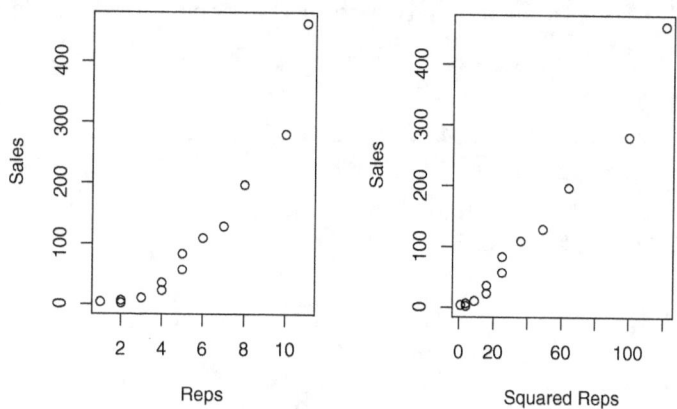

FIGURE 14.1 R plot of Manufacturing Data - Linear and Quadratic Models

```
## 
## Residuals:
##     Min      1Q  Median      3Q     Max
## -55.877  -3.523  -1.096   4.416  42.389
## 
## Coefficients:
##             Estimate Std. Error t value Pr(>|t|)
## (Intercept)  18.0642    24.6727   0.732 0.480881
## reps        -15.7208     9.5498  -1.646 0.130746
## I(reps^2)     4.7502     0.7759   6.122 0.000112 ***
## ---
## Signif. codes:  0 '***' 0.001 '**' 0.01 '*' 0.05 '.' 0.1 ' ' 1
## 
## Residual standard error: 24.59 on 10 degrees of freedom
## Multiple R-squared:  0.9726, Adjusted R-squared:  0.9672
## F-statistic: 177.8 on 2 and 10 DF,  p-value: 1.531e-08
```

Models with **interaction** terms are appropriate when the effect of one regressor on the response depends on the values of another regressor. A generic form for such a model is as follows:
$$y = \beta_0 + \beta_1 x_1 + \beta_2 x_2 + \beta_3 x_1 x_2 + \epsilon$$
In R, an interaction term is represented as in $x_1 : x_2$, but is similar to a product, not to a division. A very compact way of including all the terms in the above equation in R is $x_1 * x_2$. This peculiar syntax, however, only has this meaning (to introduce both

the linear and the interaction terms) in the R function lm(); for regular operations among vectors, the multiplication symbol has its usual meaning. Let us compare a linear model with one with an interaction term using the stock data in table 14.3 of the textbook.

```
stock1<-c(41,39,38,45,41,43,47,49,41,35,36,39,33,28,31)
stock2<-c(36,36,38,51,52,55,57,58,62,70,72,74,83,101,107)
stock3<-c(35,35,32,41,39,55,52,54,65,77,75,74,81,92,91)
lst<-lm(stock1~stock2+stock3)
summary(lst)
```

```
## 
## Call:
## lm(formula = stock1 ~ stock2 + stock3)
## 
## Residuals:
##     Min      1Q  Median      3Q     Max
## -6.0691 -2.6708 -0.9078  2.3842  8.8677
## 
## Coefficients:
##             Estimate Std. Error t value Pr(>|t|)
## (Intercept) 50.85548    3.79099  13.415 1.38e-08 ***
## stock2      -0.11900    0.19308  -0.616    0.549
## stock3      -0.07076    0.19898  -0.356    0.728
## ---
## Signif. codes:  0 '***' 0.001 '**' 0.01 '*' 0.05 '.' 0.1 ' ' 1
## 
## Residual standard error: 4.57 on 12 degrees of freedom
## Multiple R-squared:  0.4723, Adjusted R-squared:  0.3843
## F-statistic: 5.369 on 2 and 12 DF,  p-value: 0.0216
```

```
ilm<-lm(stock1~stock2*stock3)
summary(ilm)
```

```
## 
## Call:
## lm(formula = stock1 ~ stock2 * stock3)
## 
## Residuals:
```

## 14.1. NONLINEAR MODELS

```
##       Min      1Q  Median      3Q     Max
## -5.0924 -1.8280  0.1816  1.3908  5.3510
##
## Coefficients:
##                 Estimate Std. Error t value Pr(>|t|)
## (Intercept)    12.046177   9.312400   1.294  0.22232
## stock2          0.878778   0.261873   3.356  0.00641 **
## stock3          0.220493   0.143522   1.536  0.15271
## stock2:stock3  -0.009985   0.002314  -4.315  0.00123 **
## ---
## Signif. codes:  0 '***' 0.001 '**' 0.01 '*' 0.05 '.' 0.1 ' ' 1
##
## Residual standard error: 2.909 on 11 degrees of freedom
## Multiple R-squared:  0.804, Adjusted R-squared:  0.7505
## F-statistic: 15.04 on 3 and 11 DF,  p-value: 0.00033
```

The introduction of the interaction term has, in this case, significantly improved the standard error of the estimate and the $R^2$ values.

Besides transforming independent variables, one may find it useful to transform the dependent variable, $y$. The next example explores a log-linear model using data on annual sales and advertising expenditures (both in $millions). The dependent variable in a **log–linear** model is in natural logarithms, while the independent variable(s) is linear (to the power of 1), as in the following equation:

$$\log y = \beta_0 + \beta_1 x + \epsilon$$

```
sales<-c(2580,11942,9845,27800,18926,4800,14550)
advert<-c(1.2,2.6,2.2,3.2,2.9,1.5,2.7)
loglin<-lm(log(sales)~advert)
summary(loglin)
```

```
##
## Call:
## lm(formula = log(sales) ~ advert)
##
## Residuals:
##          1         2         3         4         5         6         7
## -0.135616 -0.134972  0.109539  0.053591 -0.002703  0.157005 -0.046844
##
## Coefficients:
##              Estimate Std. Error t value Pr(>|t|)
```

```
## (Intercept)   6.67834     0.16787   39.78 1.89e-07 ***
## advert        1.09402     0.06917   15.82 1.84e-05 ***
## ---
## Signif. codes:  0 '***' 0.001 '**' 0.01 '*' 0.05 '.' 0.1 ' ' 1
##
## Residual standard error: 0.1252 on 5 degrees of freedom
## Multiple R-squared:  0.9804, Adjusted R-squared:  0.9765
## F-statistic: 250.1 on 1 and 5 DF,  p-value: 1.838e-05
```

A prediction of this model at $x = x_0$ will be

$$\widehat{\log y} = b_0 + b_1 x_0$$

$$\hat{y} = e^{b_1 + b_2 x_0}$$

For example, for $advert = 2$, we can predict sales as follows:

```
advert0<-2
b0<-coef(loglin)[[1]]
b1<-coef(loglin)[[2]]
yhat<-exp(b0+b1*advert0)
cat(" Estimated sales =",round(yhat,2),"($million)" )

##  Estimated sales = 7089.54 ($million)
```

In a **log–log** model, both the dependent and the independent variables are in natural logarithms.

$$\log y = \beta_0 + \beta_1 x_1 + \epsilon$$

The predicted $\log y$ and $y$ for a given value $x_0$ are given by

$$\widehat{\log y} = b_0 + b_1 \log x_0$$

$$\hat{y} = e^{b_0 + b_1 \log x_0}$$

*Demonstration Problem 14.1*

Let us use the aerospace data to predict the dependent variable *cost* for a value of the independent variable *weight* of 3000, using a log–log model.

## 14.2. INDICATOR (DUMMY) VARIABLES

```
cost<-c(1.2,9.0,4.5,3.2,13.0,0.6,1.8,2.7) # in billions
weight<-c(450,20200,9060,3500,75600,175,800,2100) # in tons
x0<-3000
loglog<-lm(log(cost)~log(weight))
b0<-coef(loglog)[[1]]
b1<-coef(loglog)[[2]]
yhat<-exp(b0+b1*log(3000))
cat(" The predicted cost for weight =",x0,
    "tons is $",yhat, "billion")
```

```
##   The predicted cost for weight = 3000 tons is $ 2.96453 billion
```

## 14.2 Indicator (Dummy) Variables

An indicator (dummy, categorical, or qualitative) variable assigns a number (indicator) to a certain category of observations to distinguish it from the other possible categories. Indicator variables for which only two categories exist are called dichotomous (binary); when a categorical variable involves more than two categories, a binary variable is created for each of the categories. In this case, the number of binary dummy variables newly created is equal to the number of the categories in the initial categorical variable (though, technically, one of the categories will serve as a benchmark and will be excluded from the model.) A binary dummy variable is usually equal to 1 if an observation belongs to the category of interest and is equal to 0 otherwise.

*Example*: Consider the data on *salary*, *age*, and *sex*. The model to be estimated is the following:

$$salary = \beta_0 + \beta_1 age + \beta_2 M,$$

where $M$ is the $Male$ dummy variable, with $M = 1$ for men and $M = 0$ for women.

```
salary<-c(2.548,2.629,2.011,2.229,2.746,2.528,2.018,2.190,2.551,
          1.985,2.610,2.432,2.215,1.990,2.585) # in $1000
age<-c(3.2,3.8,2.7,3.4,3.6,4.1,3.8,3.4,3.3,3.2,3.5,
       2.9,3.3,2.8,3.5) # in decades
sex<-c(1,1,0,0,1,1,0,0,1,0,1,1,0,0,1) # 1 is male, 0 is female
mt145<-lm(salary~age+sex)
summary(mt145)
```

```
## 
## Call:
## lm(formula = salary ~ age + sex)
## 
## Residuals:
##       Min        1Q    Median        3Q       Max
## -0.136697 -0.067380  0.001351  0.054888  0.154863
## 
## Coefficients:
##             Estimate Std. Error t value Pr(>|t|)
## (Intercept)  1.73206    0.23558   7.352 8.83e-06 ***
## age          0.11122    0.07208   1.543    0.149
## sex          0.45868    0.05346   8.580 1.82e-06 ***
## ---
## Signif. codes:  0 '***' 0.001 '**' 0.01 '*' 0.05 '.' 0.1 ' ' 1
## 
## Residual standard error: 0.09679 on 12 degrees of freedom
## Multiple R-squared:  0.89,  Adjusted R-squared:  0.8717
## F-statistic: 48.54 on 2 and 12 DF,  p-value: 1.773e-06
```

When a dummy variable is not interacted with other variables, the dummy changes only the intercept of the regression line when moving from one category to another. Figure 14.2 shows the two parallel lines.

$$E(salary|age) = (\beta_0 + \beta_2) + \beta_1 age \text{ for men, and}$$

$$E(salary|age) = \beta_0 + \beta_1 age \text{ for women}$$

```
b0<-coef(mt145)[[1]]
b1<-coef(mt145)[[2]]
b2<-coef(mt145)[[3]]
intM<-b0+b2
intF<-b0
plot(age,salary,xlab="Age",ylab="Salary")
points(age,salary, col="blue")
abline(a=intM,b=b1,col="blue",lty=3,lwd=1)
abline(a=intF,b=b1,col="red",lty=2,lwd=1)
```

## 14.3 Model Building: Search Procedures

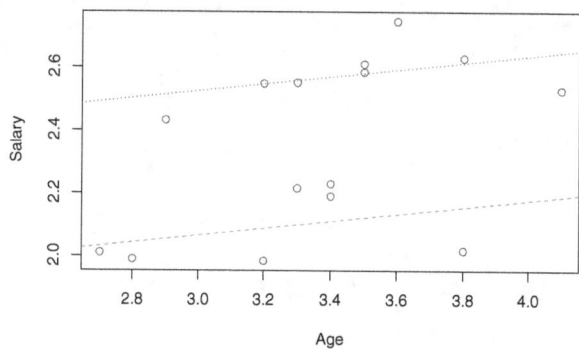

FIGURE 14.2 A Dummy that Changes Only the Intercept

## 14.3 Model Building: Search Procedures

Search procedures can be used to find a "best" model, one that fares better according to various criteria. The following example uses the Energy database, plus data on U.S. fuel rate for automobiles. The first results come from a model regressing world crude oil production on all the other variables in the dataset (see Table 14.6).

```
data("Energy", package="Black9edata")
FuelRate<-c(13.4, 13.6, 14.0, 13.8, 14.1, 14.3, 14.6, 16.0,
            16.5, 16.9, 17.1, 17.4, 17.5,17.4, 18.0, 18.8,
            19.0, 20.3, 21.2, 21.0, 20.6, 20.8, 21.1, 21.2,
            21.5, 21.6) # miles per gallon
t146<-cbind(Energy,FuelRate)
t146$Year<-NULL # removes the variable Year from the dataset
head(t146)
```

```
##   CrOilPrd USEnCons USNucGen USCoalPr USDryGas FuelRate
## 1     55.7     74.3     83.5    598.6     21.7     13.4
## 2     55.7     72.5    114.0    610.0     20.7     13.6
## 3     52.8     70.5    172.5    654.6     19.2     14.0
## 4     57.3     74.4    191.1    684.9     19.1     13.8
## 5     59.7     76.3    250.9    697.2     19.2     14.1
## 6     60.2     78.1    276.4    670.2     19.1     14.3
```

```
mt146<-lm(CrOilPrd~.,data=t146)
summary(mt146)

##
## Call:
## lm(formula = CrOilPrd ~ ., data = t146)
##
## Residuals:
##     Min      1Q  Median      3Q     Max
## -1.60006 -0.83219 -0.04438  0.95456  2.04060
##
## Coefficients:
##              Estimate Std. Error t value Pr(>|t|)
## (Intercept)  2.708466   8.908759   0.304 0.764251
## USEnCons     0.835671   0.180234   4.637 0.000159 ***
## USNucGen    -0.006544   0.009854  -0.664 0.514196
## USCoalPr     0.009825   0.007286   1.348 0.192596
## USDryGas    -0.143212   0.448408  -0.319 0.752751
## FuelRate    -0.734143   0.548823  -1.338 0.196018
## ---
## Signif. codes:  0 '***' 0.001 '**' 0.01 '*' 0.05 '.' 0.1 ' ' 1
##
## Residual standard error: 1.215 on 20 degrees of freedom
## Multiple R-squared:  0.921,  Adjusted R-squared:  0.9012
## F-statistic: 46.62 on 5 and 20 DF,  p-value: 2.409e-10
```

This model, while having impressive adjusted $R^2$ and $F$-statistic, produces only one significant variable, U.S. energy consumption. We would like to determine if there is other combination of independent variables that may produce more balanced results. This is performed by the method of step-wise regression, which in R is done by the function step(); this function uses a particular criterion of model selection, the **Akaike's Information Criterion**, AIC. The step() function can do forward selection, backward elimination, or both. Here is an example of the latter, starting from the simplest possible model (one with only an intercept and no other variables) and ending with a model that includes all variables in the dataset. The selection criterion is the AIC, which should be as small as possible for a good model.

```
novar<-lm(CrOilPrd~1,data=t146)
allvar<-lm(CrOilPrd~.,data=t146)
```

## 14.3. MODEL BUILDING: SEARCH PROCEDURES

```
step(novar, scope=list(lower=novar, upper=allvar),
     direction="both")
```

```
## Start:  AIC=71.28
## CrOilPrd ~ 1
##
##             Df Sum of Sq     RSS     AIC
## + USEnCons   1    318.31   55.12  23.537
## + USNucGen   1    168.04  205.39  57.737
## + USCoalPr   1    145.30  228.12  60.466
## + FuelRate   1    127.90  245.53  62.378
## <none>                    373.43  71.280
## + USDryGas   1     17.17  356.26  72.057
##
## Step:  AIC=23.54
## CrOilPrd ~ USEnCons
##
##             Df Sum of Sq     RSS     AIC
## + FuelRate   1     20.88   34.24  13.158
## + USNucGen   1     19.84   35.28  13.933
## + USCoalPr   1     11.35   43.77  19.545
## + USDryGas   1      9.80   45.32  20.445
## <none>                     55.12  23.537
## - USEnCons   1    318.31  373.43  71.280
##
## Step:  AIC=13.16
## CrOilPrd ~ USEnCons + FuelRate
##
##             Df Sum of Sq     RSS     AIC
## + USCoalPr   1     3.997  30.243  11.931
## <none>                    34.240  13.158
## + USDryGas   1     0.325  33.915  14.910
## + USNucGen   1     0.284  33.956  14.941
## - FuelRate   1    20.880  55.120  23.537
## - USEnCons   1   211.289 245.529  62.378
##
## Step:  AIC=11.93
## CrOilPrd ~ USEnCons + FuelRate + USCoalPr
##
##             Df Sum of Sq     RSS     AIC
## <none>                    30.243  11.931
```

```
## - USCoalPr   1     3.997  34.240 13.158
## + USNucGen   1     0.583  29.661 13.425
## + USDryGas   1     0.082  30.161 13.860
## - FuelRate   1    13.531  43.774 19.545
## - USEnCons   1   195.845 226.088 62.234

##
## Call:
## lm(formula = CrOilPrd ~ USEnCons + FuelRate + USCoalPr, data = t146)
##
## Coefficients:
## (Intercept)     USEnCons      FuelRate      USCoalPr
##     8.45414      0.75394      -1.02833       0.01048
```

The results show that the best model involves only three of the five predictors, as follows:

```
best<-lm(CrOilPrd~USEnCons+FuelRate+USCoalPr,data = t146)
sbest<-summary(best)
sbest
```

```
##
## Call:
## lm(formula = CrOilPrd ~ USEnCons + FuelRate + USCoalPr, data = t146)
##
## Residuals:
##     Min      1Q  Median      3Q     Max
## -1.5570 -0.9813  0.1836  0.9138  1.9647
##
## Coefficients:
##              Estimate Std. Error t value Pr(>|t|)
## (Intercept)  8.454140   3.462723   2.441  0.02313 *
## USEnCons     0.753943   0.063166  11.936 4.41e-11 ***
## FuelRate    -1.028331   0.327772  -3.137  0.00479 **
## USCoalPr     0.010479   0.006145   1.705  0.10225
## ---
## Signif. codes:  0 '***' 0.001 '**' 0.01 '*' 0.05 '.' 0.1 ' ' 1
##
## Residual standard error: 1.172 on 22 degrees of freedom
## Multiple R-squared:  0.919, Adjusted R-squared:  0.908
## F-statistic: 83.21 on 3 and 22 DF,  p-value: 3.659e-12
```

## 14.4 Multicollinearity

Multicollinearity arises when two or more of the regressors are highly correlated. Sometimes, a high $R^2$ but insignificant coefficients may be a sign of multicollinearity. One may examine the correlations between independent variables to assess possible multicollinearity. Here is the example of oil production data.

```
regressors<-t146
regressors$CrOilPrd<-NULL
round(cor(regressors),2)
```

```
##           USEnCons USNucGen USCoalPr USDryGas FuelRate
## USEnCons      1.00     0.86     0.79     0.06     0.79
## USNucGen      0.86     1.00     0.95    -0.40     0.97
## USCoalPr      0.79     0.95     1.00    -0.45     0.97
## USDryGas      0.06    -0.40    -0.45     1.00    -0.42
## FuelRate      0.79     0.97     0.97    -0.42     1.00
```

**Variance Inflation Factor**

John Fox's package car (Fox and Weisberg 2017) provides the function vif(), which calculates the variance inflation factor for each independent variable in a model. The function's main argument is the name of the model to be tested. The formula for the variance inflation factor corresponding to regressor $i$ is

$$VIF_i = \frac{1}{1-R_i^2},$$

where $R_i^2$ is the $R^2$ from regressing factor $i$ on all other regressors in the initial model.

```
#install.packages("car") # if not already installed
library(car)
allvar<-lm(CrOilPrd~.,data=t146)
round(vif(allvar),2)
```

```
## USEnCons USNucGen USCoalPr USDryGas FuelRate
##    20.82    61.55    21.35     6.19    42.49
```

A practical rule of thumb is that a $VIF$ greater than 10 is an indication that the respective variable may create a collinearity problem. Step-wise regression may be used to reduce multicollinearity by dropping the problematic variables from the model. The following code line identifies the regressors for which $VIF > 10$ in the oil production model.

```
vif(allvar)>10
```

```
## USEnCons USNucGen USCoalPr USDryGas FuelRate
##     TRUE     TRUE     TRUE    FALSE     TRUE
```

```
vif(best)>10
```

```
## USEnCons FuelRate USCoalPr
##    FALSE     TRUE     TRUE
```

These results show that even in the "best" model produced by step-wise regression there is still some collinearity.

## 14.5 Logistic Regression

This nonlinear model applies when the dependent variable is dichotomous (binomial), usually taking the values 0 and 1. A prediction in such a model gives the probability that the dependent variable is equal to 1, and the underlying relationship is the logistic function

$$f(x) = p = \frac{e^u}{1 + e^u},$$

$$u = \beta_0 + \beta_1 x_1 + ... + \beta_k x_k$$

Once we calculate a prediction for the probability $p$ that the event $y$ happens, we can interpret this result by calculating the odds ratio

$$S = \text{odds ratio} = \frac{p}{1-p} = e^{\beta_0 + \beta_1 x_1 + ... + \beta_k x_k}$$

Thus, the odds ratio can be easily estimated in its *logit* form,

$$\log S = \beta_0 + \beta_1 x_1 + ... + \beta_k x_k$$

The following example reproduces the auto club model (Table 14.16 in the textbook):

```
yes<-c(rep(1,36),rep(0,56))
age<-c(52,57,53,57,48,50,54,47,45,66,61,60,53,66,56,58,45,62,51,52,
       57,48,53,46,45,53,47,50,47,55,65,56,50,51,64,54,
       52,42,45,33,42,51,43,40,50,29,41,39,33,39,45,37,45,34,45,30,
       41,39,48,41,47,28,45,37,48,38,39,41,43,47,37,30,39,50,36,28,
```

## 14.5. LOGISTIC REGRESSION

```
        34,51,43,34,45,31,29,24,36,43,39,42,39,32,29,34)
dat<-data.frame(yes,age)
logit<-glm(yes~age,data=dat,family=binomial(link="logit"))
summary(logit)
```

```
## 
## Call:
## glm(formula = yes ~ age, family = binomial(link = "logit"), data = dat)
## 
## Deviance Residuals:
##     Min       1Q   Median       3Q      Max
## -1.95015  -0.32016  -0.05335   0.26538  1.72940
## 
## Coefficients:
##              Estimate Std. Error z value Pr(>|z|)
## (Intercept) -20.40782    4.52332  -4.512 6.43e-06 ***
## age           0.42592    0.09482   4.492 7.05e-06 ***
## ---
## Signif. codes:  0 '***' 0.001 '**' 0.01 '*' 0.05 '.' 0.1 ' ' 1
## 
## (Dispersion parameter for binomial family taken to be 1)
## 
##     Null deviance: 123.156  on 91  degrees of freedom
## Residual deviance:  49.937  on 90  degrees of freedom
## AIC: 53.937
## 
## Number of Fisher Scoring iterations: 7
```

```
anova(logit)
```

```
## Analysis of Deviance Table
## 
## Model: binomial, link: logit
## 
## Response: yes
## 
## Terms added sequentially (first to last)
## 
## 
##      Df Deviance Resid. Df Resid. Dev
## NULL                    91    123.156
```

## age        1    73.22        90      49.937

The regression results can be used to predict the probability that a person of a given age will request additional information (i.e., $y =$"Yes"); the function predict(), with the model name as a first argument and type="response" as a second argument achieves this. The next code lines calculate this prediction, as well as the odds ratio.

```
newage<-data.frame(age=50)
phat<-predict(logit,newdata=newage,type="response")
oddshat<-phat/(1-phat)
cat("  Prob. of 'yes' for age=50 is ",round(phat,3),"\n",
    " Odds ratio =",round(oddshat,3))

##    Prob. of 'yes' for age=50 is  0.708
##    Odds ratio = 2.43
```

# Chapter 15

# Time Series Forecasting

Time series data measure a characteristic of the population at fixed time intervals over extended periods.

## 15.1 Introduction to Forecasting

The **time-$t$ forecast error** is the difference ($e_t$) between the actual ($x_t$) and the forecasted ($F_t$) values of the variable under consideration.

$$e_t = x_t - F_t$$

The **mean absolute deviation** over a number of forecasts is given by the formula:

$$MAD = \frac{\sum |e_i|}{\text{Number of forecasts}}$$

*Example: Nonfarm Partnership Tax Return* (Table 15.2, textbook). In this example, we have a missing value in the first row of the forecast. Therefore, we will use the function `is.na()` to identify the missing value (`NA`) and then select only the rows for which the forecast is not missing. The number of forecasts is determined by the function `NROW()`, which gives the number of observations in the dataset after eliminating the rows corresponding to the missing values.

```
y<-1:11
x<-c(1402,1458,1553,1613,1676,1755,1807,1824,1826,1780,1759)
f<-c(NA, 1402,1441.2,1519.5,1585.0,1648.7,1723.1,1781.8,1811.3,
     1821.6,1792.5)
```

```
df<-data.frame(y,x,f)
df1<-df[is.na(df$f)==FALSE,]
MAD<-sum(abs(df1$x-df1$f))/NROW(df1)
cat("  MAD =",MAD)
```

```
##    MAD = 67.45
```

The mean square error of the forecast is given by

$$MSE = \frac{\sum e_i^2}{\text{Number of forecasts}}$$

```
MSE<-sum((df1$x-df1$f)^2)/NROW(df1)
cat("  MSE =",MSE)
```

```
##    MSE = 5584.713
```

## 15.2 Smoothing Techniques

R constructs time series by using the function ts(data,start,end,frequency), where data is a vector or a matrix of observations. The functions lag() and diff() create lagged and differenced time series, with the caveat that a negative lag $-k$ moves the time series $k$ periods forward (i.e., $lag_{-1}(x_t) = x_{t-1}$). The next code shows how to construct and plot a time series and its one-period lag. The plot is shown in Figure 15.1.

```
bell<-c(336,308,582,771,935,808,663,380,333,412,458,412)
bell.ts<-ts(bell,start=c(1,1),end=c(1,12),frequency=12)
bell.ts
```

```
##     Jan Feb Mar Apr May Jun Jul Aug Sep Oct Nov Dec
## 1   336 308 582 771 935 808 663 380 333 412 458 412
```

```
plot.ts(bell.ts,type="o",pch=16, ylab="Shipments")
```

Forecasting by **simple average** calculates the next period's forecast by averaging over a number of previous periods. For example, let us forecast the price of natural gas for June of year 3 by averaging the prices over the previous 12 months (from June of year 2 to May of year 3). The function window() extracts a subset of observations from a time series, one defined by its starting and ending dates. A date in a time series

## 15.2. SMOOTHING TECHNIQUES

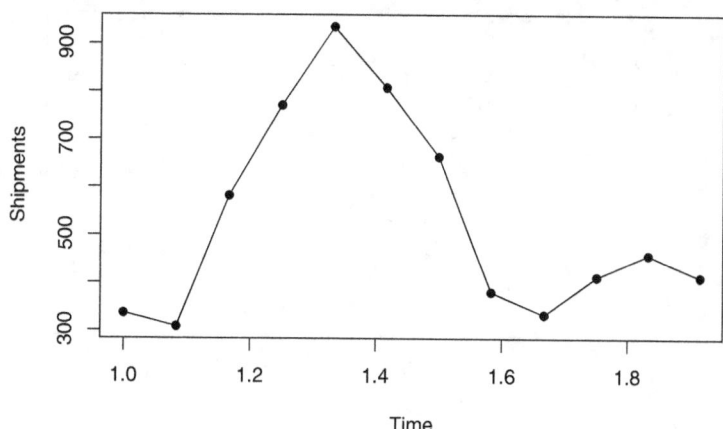

FIGURE 15.1 R Graph of Shipments of Bell Peppers over 12 Months

is given under the form c(period_unit,subperiod), such as c(year,month), or c(year,quarter). Figure 15.2 shows the plot.

```
price<-c(4.5,4.04,4.07,4.27,4.34,4.52,4.35,3.98,3.85,3.62,3.56,3.25,
         2.71,2.53,2.3,2.05,2.49,2.5,2.96,2.81,2.92,3.5,3.69,3.44,
         3.35,3.31,3.77,4.16,4.07)
price.ts<-ts(price,start=c(1,1),end=c(3,5),frequency=12) #monthly
plot.ts(price.ts,type="o",pch=16, ylab="Price")

# The simple average forecast for June, year 3:
f<-mean(window(price.ts,start=c(2,6),end=c(3,5)))
cat("Simple average forecast for June of year 3 =",round(f,2))
```

## Simple average forecast for June of year 3 = 3.37

A $k$-period **moving average** is the average of the variable under consideration over the previous $k$ periods preceding the forecasting date; thus, when the forecasting date changes, the averaging period set (*window*) changes. The R function filter(x,k) calculates univariate moving average forecasts using a moving window of $k$ periods. Figure 15.3 shows the actual shipments series and a 4-period moving average forecast.

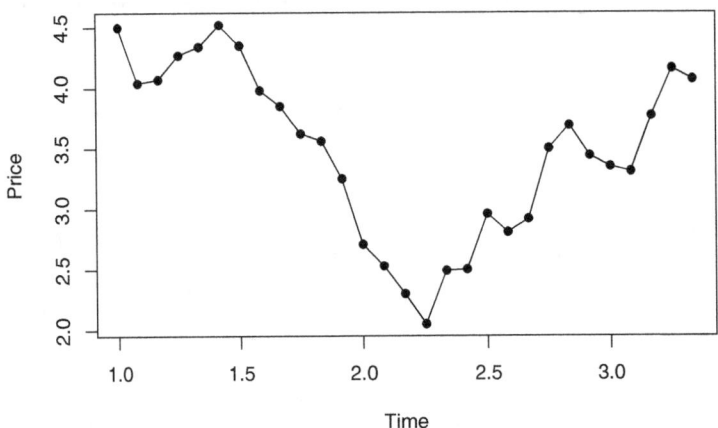

FIGURE 15.2 R Graph of Natural Gas Futures Data

```
shipments<-c(1056,1345,1381,1191,1259,1361,1110,1334,1416,1282,
        1341,1382)
k=4 # the number of past periods to include
weights=c(0,rep(1/k,k))
ship.ts=ts(shipments,start=c(1,1),end=c(1,12),frequency=12)#monthly
fship.ts<-filter(ship.ts,filter=weights,sides=1)#forecasts
ts.plot(ship.ts,fship.ts,lty=c(1,2),col=c("red","blue"),type="o",
        ylab="Shipment")
legend("bottomright",c("Actual","Forecasted"),lty=c(1,2),
     col=c("red","blue"))

errors1<-ship.ts-fship.ts
```

There are a few novelties in the above code sequence. First, the function filter() includes the argument filter, which is a vector of weights for each period in the window, plus a weight for the contemporaneous observation. I chose the weights to be 0 for the first forecasted date, and equal to $1/4$ for all four past periods; the argument sides is equal to 1, to tell R to take the moving average periods only from one side of the time series (in this case only *before* the first forecasted date). Last, the function ts.plot() plots two or more time series on the same graph; the function legend() creates a legend for a previously constructed plot.

When the weights are different for different periods in the moving average window, the

## 15.2. SMOOTHING TECHNIQUES

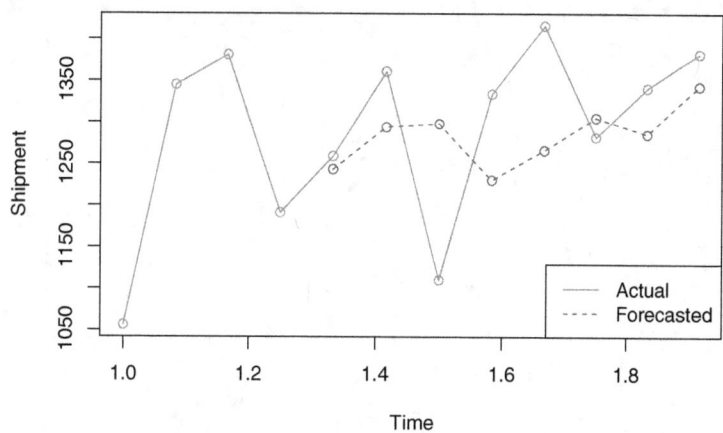

FIGURE 15.3 R Plot of the Shipment and Forecasted Time Series

method is called **weighted moving average**. Let us apply different weights in the shipment example.

*Demonstration Problem 15.2*: Weighted Moving Average

The forecasted series with weighted moving average is presented in Figure 15.4.

```
shipments<-c(1056,1345,1381,1191,1259,1361,1110,1334,1416,1282,
             1341,1382)
weights=c(0,4/8,2/8,1/8,1/8)
ship.ts=ts(shipments,start=c(1,1),end=c(1,12),frequency=12)
fship.ts<-filter(ship.ts,filter=weights,sides=1) #forecasts
ts.plot(ship.ts,fship.ts,lty=c(1,2),col=c("red","blue"),type="o")
legend("bottomright",c("Actual","Forecasted"),lty=c(1,2),
       col=c("red","blue"))
```

```
errors2<-ship.ts-fship.ts
```

```
dfr<-data.frame(ship.ts,errors1,errors2)
names(dfr)<-c("Shipments","Error1", "Error2")
dfr
```

```
##     Shipments   Error1    Error2
## 1        1056       NA        NA
```

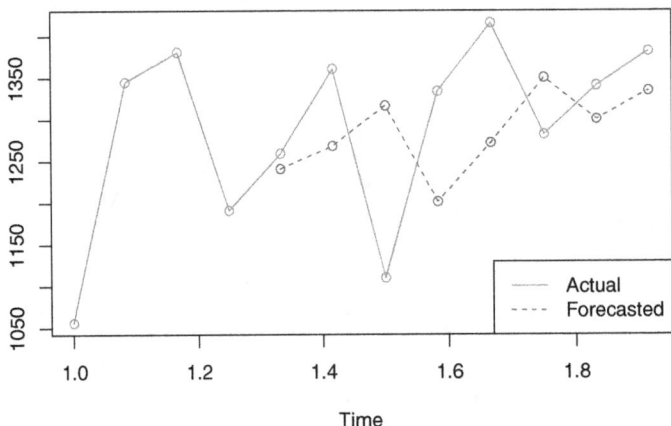

FIGURE 15.4 Forecasted Shipments, with Weighted Moving Average

```
## 2     1345      NA        NA
## 3     1381      NA        NA
## 4     1191      NA        NA
## 5     1259    15.75    18.125
## 6     1361    67.00    93.000
## 7     1110  -188.00  -206.750
## 8     1334   103.75   132.500
## 9     1416   150.00   144.000
## 10    1282   -23.25   -68.375
## 11    1341    55.50    40.500
## 12    1382    38.75    47.250
```

Another forecasting method is **exponential smoothing**; the forecasted (time $t+1$) level is a weighted average between the current (time $t$) level and the forecasted level for the current period. The weights are, respectively, $\alpha$, which is called the exponential smoothing constant, and, unsurprisingly, $(1-\alpha)$.

$$F_{t+1} = \alpha X_t + (1-\alpha) F_t$$

*Demonstration Problem 15.3*: U.S. Housing Data

First, we construct the time series and plot the data; Figure 15.5 shows this graph.

## 15.2. SMOOTHING TECHNIQUES

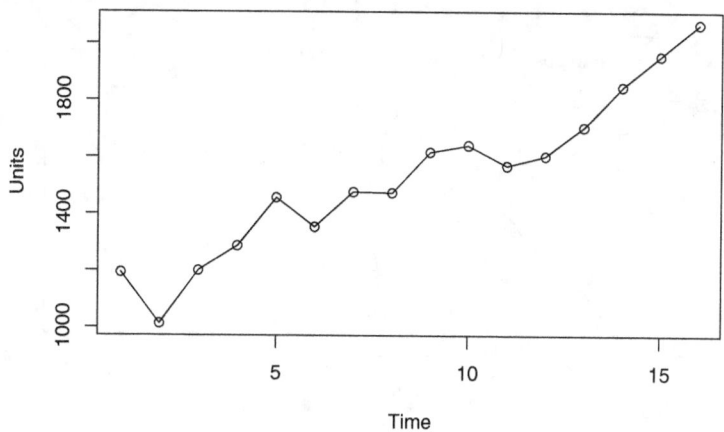

FIGURE 15.5 Time Series Plot for Demonstration Problem 15.3

```
units<-c(1193,1014,1200,1288,1457,1354,1477,1474,1617,1641,
         1569,1603,1705,1848,1956,2068)
units.ts<-ts(units,start=1,end=16,frequency=1) #annual data
ts.plot(units.ts,type="o", ylab="Units")
```

Then, we apply the HoltWinters() function to the time series, extract the forecasted series from the HoltWinters object, and plot the results. Figure 15.6 shows the actual series and the forecasted series for $\alpha = 0.2$, $0.5$, and $0.8$.

```
fHW2<-HoltWinters(units.ts,alpha=0.2,beta=FALSE,gamma=FALSE)
f02<-fHW2$fitted
e02<-units.ts-f02
MAD02<-sum(abs(e02))/length(e02)
MSE02<-sum(e02^2)/length(e02)
fHW5<-HoltWinters(units.ts,alpha=0.5,beta=FALSE,gamma=FALSE)
f05<-fHW5$fitted
e05<-units.ts-f05
MAD05<-sum(abs(e05))/length(e05)
MSE05<-sum(e05^2)/length(e05)
fHW8<-HoltWinters(units.ts,alpha=0.8,beta=FALSE,gamma=FALSE)
f08<-fHW8$fitted
e08<-units.ts-f08
```

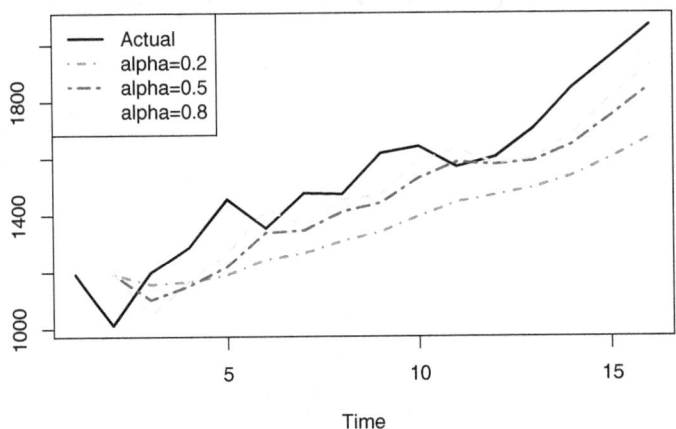

FIGURE 15.6 Actual and Forecasted Series for Demonstration Problem 15.3

```
MAD08<-sum(abs(e08))/length(e08)
MSE08<-sum(e08^2)/length(e08)
tsu<-ts.union(units.ts,f02[,2],f05[,2],f08[,2])
ts.plot(tsu,col=c("black","red","blue","green"),
        lty=c(1,4,6,8),lwd=rep(2,4))
legend("topleft",c("Actual","alpha=0.2","alpha=0.5","alpha=0.8"),
        col=c("black","red","blue","green"),
        lty=c(1,4,6,8),lwd=rep(2,4))
```

Finally, we can construct a table showing the results for the three values of $\alpha$.

```
tsu1<-ts.union(units.ts,f02[,2],e02[,2],f05[,2],e05[,2],f08[,2],
               e08[,2],dframe=TRUE)
tsu1<-round(tsu1,1)
names(tsu1)<-c("Actual","F02","e02","F05","e05","F08","e08")
tsu1
```

```
##     Actual    F02     e02    F05     e05    F08     e08
## 1     1193     NA      NA     NA      NA     NA      NA
## 2     1014 1193.0  -179.0 1193.0  -179.0 1193.0  -179.0
## 3     1200 1157.2    42.8 1103.5    96.5 1049.8   150.2
## 4     1288 1165.8   122.2 1151.8   136.2 1170.0   118.0
```

## 15.3. TREND ANALYSIS

```
## 5     1457 1190.2  266.8 1219.9  237.1 1264.4  192.6
## 6     1354 1243.6  110.4 1338.4   15.6 1418.5  -64.5
## 7     1477 1265.7  211.3 1346.2  130.8 1366.9  110.1
## 8     1474 1307.9  166.1 1411.6   62.4 1455.0   19.0
## 9     1617 1341.1  275.9 1442.8  174.2 1470.2  146.8
## 10    1641 1396.3  244.7 1529.9  111.1 1587.6   53.4
## 11    1569 1445.2  123.8 1585.5  -16.5 1630.3  -61.3
## 12    1603 1470.0  133.0 1577.2   25.8 1581.3   21.7
## 13    1705 1496.6  208.4 1590.1  114.9 1598.7  106.3
## 14    1848 1538.3  309.7 1647.6  200.4 1683.7  164.3
## 15    1956 1600.2  355.8 1747.8  208.2 1815.1  140.9
## 16    2068 1671.4  396.6 1851.9  216.1 1927.8  140.2
cat("   MAD02 =",MAD02,"   MAD05 =",MAD05,"   MAD08 =",MAD08,"\n",
    "  MSE02 =",MSE02,"  MSE05 =",MSE05,"  MSE08 =",MSE08)

##    MAD02 = 209.7676    MAD05 = 128.3194    MAD08 = 111.2213
##   MSE02 = 53110.57    MSE05 = 21629.51    MSE08 = 15245.91
```

## 15.3 Trend Analysis

A first method we investigate is **linear regression** with time series.

$$y_i = \beta_0 + \beta_1 x_{ti} + \epsilon_i,$$

where the subscript $x_t$ denotes the variable *time*, and $i$ is the period, $i = 1, ..., T$. The expected value of $y$ generated by this model represents the equation of the trend,

$$E(y_i) = \beta_0 + \beta_1 x_{ti}$$

Figure 15.7 shows the linear trend model for the workweek data.

```
hours<-c(37.2,37.0,37.4,37.5,37.7,37.7,37.4,37.2,37.3,37.2,36.9,
36.7,36.7,36.5,36.3,35.9,35.8,35.9,36.0,35.7,35.6,35.2,34.8,35.3,35.6,
35.6,35.6,35.9,36.0,35.7,35.7,35.5,35.6,36.3,36.5)
x<-1:35
mhours<-lm(hours~x)
shours<-summary(mhours)
plot(x,hours,type="o",col="brown",xlab="Period", ylab="Hours")
abline(mhours)
```

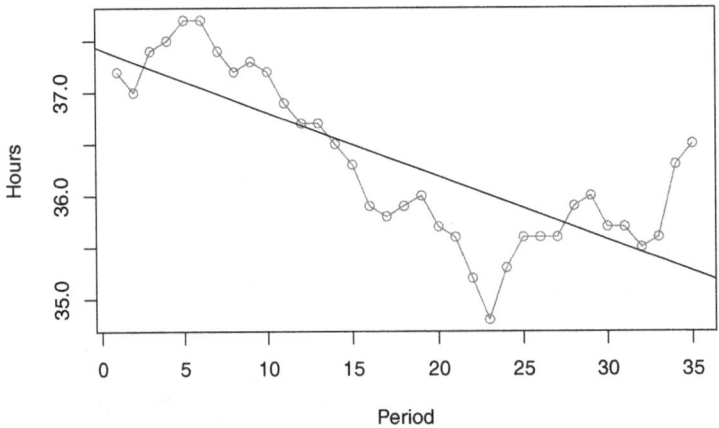

FIGURE 15.7 The Workweek Example with Linear Trend

Predicted values for the 23rd and 41st periods can be calculated as follows:

```
newx<-data.frame(x=c(23,41))
yhat<-predict(mhours,newdata=newx)
cat(" The predicted value for hours for period",newx[1,1],"is",
      yhat[1],"\n","The predicted value for hours for period",
      newx[2,1],"is",yhat[2])
```

```
## The predicted value for hours for period 23 is 36.00457
## The predicted value for hours for period 41 is 34.89986
```

When the linear trend does not seem to accurately model the data, one may use a **quadratic regression** model,

$$y_i = \beta_0 + \beta_1 x_{ti} + \beta_2 x_{ti}^2 + \epsilon_i.$$

The next code lines estimate such a model; the corresponding graph is shown in Figure 15.8.

```
mqh<-lm(hours~x+I(x^2))
yhatq<-predict(mqh)
plot(x,hours,col="dark orange",pch=16,
     xlab="Period (Year)",ylab="Hours Worked per Week")
```

## 15.4. SEASONAL EFFECTS

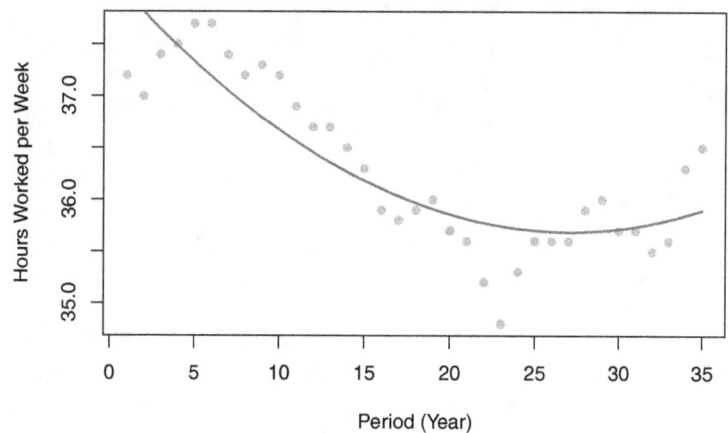

FIGURE 15.8 Quadratic Trend for the Workweek Example

```
lines(x,yhatq,col="brown",lwd=2)
```

## 15.4 Seasonal Effects

Figure 15.9 shows a plot of the household appliances data; the next code lines reproduce the textbook Table 15.8 following the step-by-step procedure explained in the textbook.

```
appliances<-c(4009,4321,4224,3944,4123,4522,4657,4030,4493,4806,
              4551,4485,4595,4799,4417,4258,4245,4900,4585,4533)
tsap<-ts(appliances,start=c(1,1),end=c(5,4),frequency=4)
ts.plot(tsap,type="o", ylab="Appliances")

weights=c(rep(1/4,4))
fourQmt<-4*filter(tsap,filter=weights,sides=2);fourQmt
```

```
##     Qtr1  Qtr2  Qtr3  Qtr4
## 1     NA 16498 16612 16813
## 2  17246 17332 17702 17986
## 3  17880 18335 18437 18430
## 4  18296 18069 17719 17820
```

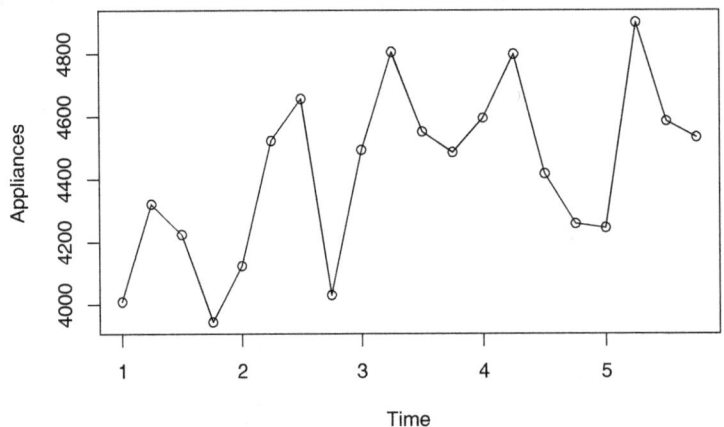

FIGURE 15.9 R plot of Household Appliances Time Series

```
## 5  17988  18263    NA     NA
fourQ2Ymt<-filter(fourQmt,filter=c(1,1),sides=2);fourQ2Ymt

##     Qtr1  Qtr2  Qtr3  Qtr4
## 1     NA 33110 33425 34059
## 2  34578 35034 35688 35866
## 3  36215 36772 36867 36726
## 4  36365 35788 35539 35808
## 5  36251    NA    NA    NA
TC<-fourQ2Ymt/8
SI<-lag(tsap,1)/TC*100 #the lag syncronizes the series
tsu<-data.frame(round(ts.union(tsap,fourQmt,fourQ2Ymt,TC,SI),2))
TCI<-TC
names(tsu)<-c("Actual","4-Q MT","4-Q, 2-Y MT","TC","SI")
tsu

##     Actual 4-Q MT 4-Q, 2-Y MT      TC     SI
## 1     4009     NA          NA      NA     NA
## 2     4321  16498       33110 4138.75 102.06
## 3     4224  16612       33425 4178.12  94.40
## 4     3944  16813       34059 4257.38  96.84
## 5     4123  17246       34578 4322.25 104.62
```

## 15.4. SEASONAL EFFECTS

```
## 6    4522  17332    35034 4379.25 106.34
## 7    4657  17702    35688 4461.00  90.34
## 8    4030  17986    35866 4483.25 100.22
## 9    4493  17880    36215 4526.88 106.17
## 10   4806  18335    36772 4596.50  99.01
## 11   4551  18437    36867 4608.38  97.32
## 12   4485  18430    36726 4590.75 100.09
## 13   4595  18296    36365 4545.62 105.57
## 14   4799  18069    35788 4473.50  98.74
## 15   4417  17719    35539 4442.38  95.85
## 16   4258  17820    35808 4476.00  94.84
## 17   4245  17988    36251 4531.38 108.13
## 18   4900  18263       NA      NA     NA
## 19   4585    NA       NA      NA     NA
## 20   4533    NA       NA      NA     NA
```

In R, time series can be decomposed in trend and seasonal effects using the function decompose(), which can also be combined with plot(). The following code is based on the same data as before, the household appliance data, with the decomposition shown in Figure 15.10.

```
tsDec<-decompose(tsap,type="mult")
TC<-tsDec$trend    # trend, as in column 5 of Table 15.8 textbook
SI<-tsDec$seasonal # seasonal indexes, as in Table 15.10 textbook
plot(decompose(tsap,type="mult"))
```

Figure 15.11 shows seasonal fluctuations superimposed on trend.

```
ts.plot(cbind(TC,TC*SI),col=c("blue","red"),type="o",
        ylab="Appliances")
cat("Seasonal indexes are:", round(100*unique(SI),2))
```

```
## Seasonal indexes are: 97.96 106.09 101.5 94.44
```

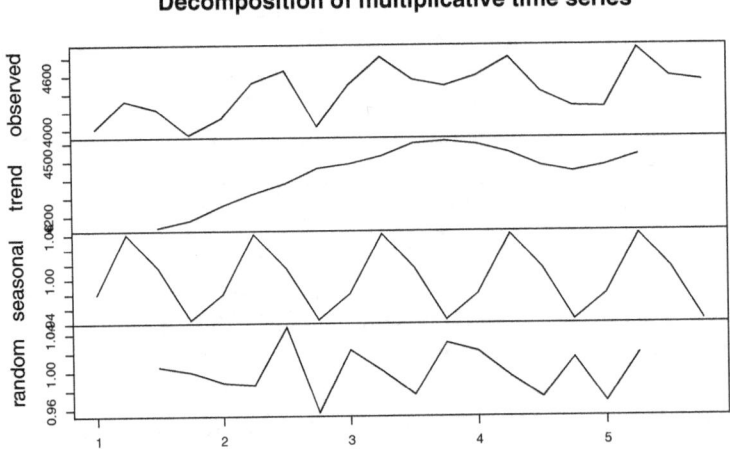

FIGURE 15.10 Decomposition of Household Appliances in Trend and Seasonal Effects

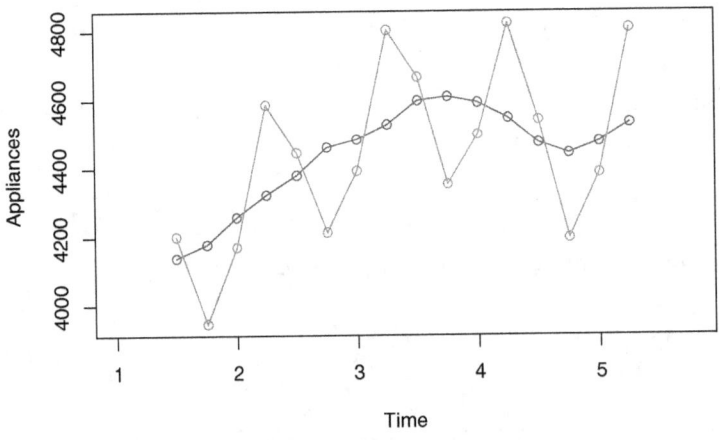

FIGURE 15.11 Seasonal Fluctuations and Trend

## 15.5 Autocorrelation and Autoregression

Autocorrelation, or **serial correlation** occurs when a period's level of a time series variable is correlated to past periods' levels. In particular, autocorrelation is important in error term series associates with a time series regression, because serially correlated errors violate regression assumptions. First-order autocorrelation can be modeled as a relationship between a contemporaneous error and its one-period lag, as follows:

$$e_t = \rho e_{t-1} + \nu_t$$

This relationship is the base for the Durbin Watson test, which concerns the hypothesis

$$H_0 : \rho = 0 \quad H_a : \rho > 0$$

The Durbin–Watson statistic to test this hypothesis is

$$D = \frac{\sum_{t=2}^{n} (e_t - e_{t-1})^2}{\sum_{t=1}^{n} e_t^2}$$

Here is the example of U.S. crude oil production and natural gas withdrawals, for which Table 15.2 in the textbook provides 25-year data. The underlying regression model is the following (small differences from the textbook results come from rounding errors):

$$gas_t = \beta_0 + \beta_1 oil_t + \epsilon_t$$

```
oil<-c(8.597,8.572,8.649,8.688,8.879,8.971,8.680,8.349,8.140,7.613,
       7.355,7.417,7.171,6.847,6.662,6.560,6.465,6.452,6.252,5.881,
       5.822,5.801,5.746,5.681,5.430)# in 1000s
gas<-c(17.573,17.337,15.809,14.153,15.513,14.535,14.154,14.807,
       15.467,15.709,16.054,16.018,16.165,16.691,17.351,17.282,
       17.373,17.844,17.729,17.590,17.726,18.129,17.795,17.819,
       17.739) #in 1000s
oil<-ts(oil)
gas<-ts(gas)
mgas<-lm(gas~oil)
res<-ts(resid(mgas))
numerator<-sum((res-lag(res,-1))^2)
denom<-sum(res^2)
D=numerator/denom
cat(" Durbin-Watson statistic D =",D)
```

```
##  Durbin-Watson statistic D = 0.7029445
```

The R function `dwtest()` in package `lmtest` calculates the Durbin–Watson statistic for a data series, producing both the test statistic and its $p$-value. Here is the code for applying this function to the residual series from the gas-oil regression model.

```
# install.packages("lmtest") # if not installed
library(lmtest)
dw<-dwtest(mgas,alternative="greater")
dw

##
##  Durbin-Watson test
##
## data:  mgas
## DW = 0.70294, p-value = 2.945e-05
## alternative hypothesis: true autocorrelation is greater than 0
```

The autocorrelation test we have just performed came out positive; thus, we need to find a solution to eliminate autocorrelation in the errors. One way is to include **autoregressive** terms in our model, which are lags of the response variable; the maximum lag included gives the *order* of the autoregressive model. The following equation shows a generic autoregressive model of order two.

$$y_t = \beta_0 + \beta_1 y_{t-1} + \beta_2 y_{t-2} + \nu_t$$

Let us construct an autoregressive model of order two to forecast natural gas withdrawals.

```
gasl1<-lag(gas,-1)
gasl2<-lag(gas,-2)
gas2<-ts.union(gas, gasl1,gasl2) #to syncronize the series
mgasAR<-lm(gas~gasl1+gasl2,data=gas2)
summary(mgasAR)

##
## Call:
## lm(formula = gas ~ gasl1 + gasl2, data = gas2)
##
## Residuals:
##      Min       1Q   Median       3Q      Max
## -1.60021 -0.09097  0.09917  0.32892  1.18503
##
## Coefficients:
```

## 15.5. AUTOCORRELATION AND AUTOREGRESSION

```
##              Estimate Std. Error t value Pr(>|t|)
## (Intercept)    2.4558     1.9817   1.239 0.229597
## gasl1          0.9642     0.2222   4.340 0.000318 ***
## gasl2         -0.1122     0.2240  -0.501 0.621945
## ---
## Signif. codes:  0 '***' 0.001 '**' 0.01 '*' 0.05 '.' 0.1 ' ' 1
##
## Residual standard error: 0.6935 on 20 degrees of freedom
##   (4 observations deleted due to missingness)
## Multiple R-squared:  0.7413, Adjusted R-squared:  0.7154
## F-statistic: 28.65 on 2 and 20 DF,  p-value: 1.345e-06
```

# Chapter 16

# Analysis with Categorical Data

Categorical data are frequency counts along one or several dimensions. Such data are often analyzed with chi-square methods, such as the chi-square goodness-of-fit test and the chi-square test of independence.

## 16.1 Chi-Square Goodness-of-Fit Test

The chi-square goodness-of-fit test concerns multinomial distributions of only one variable; its test statistic is given by the formula

$$\chi^2 = \sum \frac{(f_0 - f_e)^2}{f_e},$$

$$df = k - 1 - c$$

where

- $f_0$ = frequency of observed values
- $f_e$ = frequency of expected values
- $k$ = number of categories
- $c$ = number of parameters to be estimated

Given a reference (expected) set of numbers, the $\chi^2$ goodness-of-fit test seeks to determine if another set, the measured one, belongs to the same distribution as the reference set. Example: A national survey generates the set of count numbers (frequencies) $(16.56, 97.29, 70.38, 22.77)$, while a sub-population generates the set $(21, 109, 62, 15)$. The question is, is the distribution the same in the sub-population as the one in the national survey? The hypothesis to be tested is.

$H_0$ : The observed distribution is the same as the expected one

$H_a$ : The observed distribution is not the same as the expected one

Let us reproduce the example in Tables 16.2 and 16.3 in the textbook. In this case, $c = 0$ since the distribution is given, it does not need to be estimated. For each of the next examples, the test is conducted using, first, the textbook method, then the chisq.test() function that is available in base R.

```
refPerc<-c(.08,.47,.34,.11)
obsFreq<-c(21,109,62,15)
c<-0
tFreq<-sum(obsFreq) # total number of subjects in sub-population
k<-length(refPerc)
df<-k-1-c
refFreq<-refPerc*tFreq # reference frequencies
statistic<-sum((obsFreq-refFreq)^2/refFreq)
pval<-1-pchisq(statistic,df)
cat(" Chi-square statistic =",statistic," p-value =",pval)
```

```
##  Chi-square statistic = 6.249084    p-value = 0.100101
```

```
# Using R's chisq.test() function
chisq.test(obsFreq,p=refPerc)
```

```
## 
##  Chi-squared test for given probabilities
## 
## data:  obsFreq
## X-squared = 6.2491, df = 3, p-value = 0.1001
```

*Demonstration Problem 16.1:* Testing for Uniform Distribution

Is a given set of numbers consistent with a uniform distribution? A uniform distribution has the same frequencies in all categories. The expected distribution involves equal numbers in the set; in other words, each expected observation should be equal to the average of all actual observations.

$H_0$ : Distribution is uniform

$H_a$ : Distribution is not uniform

## 16.1. CHI-SQUARE GOODNESS-OF-FIT TEST

```
obsFreq<-c(1610,1585,1649,1590,1540,1397,1410,1350,1495,1564,
         1602,1655)
c<-0
dg<-length(obsFreq)-1-c
tFreq<-sum(obsFreq)
refFreq<-rep(tFreq/length(obsFreq),length(obsFreq))
statistic<-sum((obsFreq-refFreq)^2/refFreq)
pval<-1-pchisq(statistic,dg)
cat(" Chi-square statistic =",statistic," p-value =",pval)

##  Chi-square statistic = 74.37583    p-value = 1.78545e-11
chisq.test(obsFreq)

## 
##  Chi-squared test for given probabilities
## 
## data:  obsFreq
## X-squared = 74.376, df = 11, p-value = 1.785e-11
```

The result suggests rejecting the null hypothesis of uniform distribution.

The chisq.test() function accepts the following main arguments, according to its documentation:

- x, a numeric vector or matrix of observed data. If x is a vector and y is not given, R performs a goodness-of-fit test. In this case, the hypothesis tested is whether the population probabilities equal those in p, or are all equal if p is not given.
- y, a numeric vector, which is ignored if x is a matrix. If x is a factor, y should be a factor of the same length.
- p, a vector of probabilities of the same length as x

*Demonstration Problem 16.2:* Testing for Poisson Distribution

A Poisson distribution is determined by the parameter $\lambda$, the average arrival rate over a given interval. We would like to test that a set of data follows a Poisson distribution and to estimate its $\lambda$.

$$H_0 : \text{The data follows a Poisson distribution}$$

$$H_a : \text{The data does not follow a Poisson distribution}$$

Since $\lambda$, the parameter of the distribution, is unknown, we need to estimate it from the data, assuming that the data indeed has a Poisson distribution. We know that, for a Poisson distribution, $\lambda$ is the mean of the distribution. Therefore, we set it equal to the average number of arrivals per observation in the data.

Let us say we consider six categories, each characterized by the possible number of arrivals per period of observation, $a = (0, 1, 2, 3, 4, 5)$. Let us also denote by $x$ the vector of count data, in which each element is the number of times a category has been observed. For example, if we have observed a total of 84 periods and during 18 of these there were 0 arrivals, then the first element of the vector $x$, the one corresponding to the category of 0 arrivals, is 18. Then $\lambda$, the average number of arrivals per period of observation, is given by

$$\hat{\lambda} = \frac{\sum_{i=1}^{6} a_i x_i}{\sum_{i=1}^{6} x_i}$$

Once $\lambda$ is estimated, we can construct a vector of (expected) probabilities using the (just estimated) Poisson distribution, one probability for each category, that is, for each number of arrivals as in the given data.

```
a<-c(0,1,2,3,4,5) # vector of categories, possible arrivals per period
x<-c(7,18,25,17,12,5)# vector of count numbers for each category
sum_ax<-sum(a*x)
sum_x<-sum(x)
lambda<-sum_ax/sum_x # estimated lambda
p<-dpois(a,lambda)# expected probabilities
p[6]<-1-ppois(4,lambda)# p[6] is the prob. arrivals >= 5, i.e, arr. >4
chisq.test(x,p=p)
```

```
## 
##  Chi-squared test for given probabilities
## 
## data:  x
## X-squared = 1.7788, df = 5, p-value = 0.8788
```

Result: We do not reject $H_0$: "Data follows a Poisson distribution."

## 16.2 Chi-Square Test of Independence

The **chi-square test of independence** seeks to determine if two or more categorical variables are independent, using the observed numbers of occurrences in each combination of categories, one category for each variable. For two categorical variables, the

## 16.2. CHI-SQUARE TEST OF INDEPENDENCE

count data can be organized in a **contingency** table, which can be normalized to become a joint probability table by dividing the frequency shown in each cell by the sum of all frequency counts. If the variables are independent, one would expect that the cell (joint) probability be equal to the product of the marginal probabilities.

The test statistic is given by

$$\chi^2 = \sum \sum \frac{(f_o - f_e)^2}{f_e}$$

$$df = (r-1)(c-1)$$

where

- $r =$ number of rows
- $c =$ number of columns
- $f_o =$ frequency of observed values
- $f_e =$ frequency of expected values

The hypothesis to be tested is

$$H_0 : \text{The variables are independent}$$

$$H_a : \text{The variables are related}$$

The following example concerns two variables: type of gasoline, with three categories (regular, premium, extra), and a person's income, divided in four intervals (low, lmed, hmed, high). We would like to test if these two variables are independent. While R can be useful if these calculations are done step by step, the fastest way is to use the same function chisq.test() as we have encountered before. The frequencies should be provided under the form of a matrix, which can be constructed using the functions rbind() if data is introduced left-to-right row by row, or cbind() if the data is introduced up-to-bottom, column by column.

```
x<-rbind(c(85,16,6),
         c(102,27,13),
         c(36,22,15),
         c(15,23,25))
chisq.test(x)

## 
##  Pearson's Chi-squared test
## 
## data:  x
## X-squared = 70.727, df = 6, p-value = 2.9e-13
```

Our test rejects the hypothesis of independence between the type of gasoline purchased and a person's income.

*Demonstration Problem 16.3:* Type of Beverage vs. Age

```
x<-rbind(c(26,95,18),
         c(41,40,20),
         c(24,13,32))
chisq.test(x)

## 
##  Pearson's Chi-squared test
## 
## data:  x
## X-squared = 59.405, df = 4, p-value = 3.869e-12
```

# Chapter 17

# Nonparametric Statistics

Many nonparametric techniques make no assumptions about the distribution of a variable in the population. Such techniques are useful with nominal or ordinal data.

## 17.1 Runs Test

The runs test determines whether the sequence of observations in a sample is random. The hypothesis tested by a one-sample runs tests is

$H_0$ : The observations in the sample are randomly generated

$H_a$ : The observations are not randomly generated

One of the functions that performs dichotomous (binary) runs tests in R is the function `runs.test()` in package `tseries`. The main argument of the function is the data vector we want to test, but it first needs to be declared as `factor`.

```
#install.packages("tseries") #if not installed
library(tseries)
cola<-c("d","c","c","c","c","c","d","c","c","d","c","c","c","c",
        "d","c","d","c","c","c","d","d","d","c","c","c")
x<-factor(cola)
runs.test(x)

##
##  Runs Test
```

```
## 
## data:  x
## Standard Normal = -0.036404, p-value = 0.971
## alternative hypothesis: two.sided
```

Here is an example of large-size sample. The `runs.test()` function, however, does not require the user to specify whether the sample is large or small.

```
fn<-c("n","n","n","f","n","n","n","n","n","n","n","f", "n","n",
      "f","f","n","n","n","n","n","n", "f","n","n","n","n", "f",
      "n","n","n","n","n","n","f","f","f","f","n","n","n","n","n",
      "n","n","n","n","n","n","n")
x<-factor(fn)
runs.test(x)
```

```
## 
##  Runs Test
## 
## data:  x
## Standard Normal = -1.8074, p-value = 0.0707
## alternative hypothesis: two.sided
```

## 17.2 Mann–Whitney U Test

This nonparametric test determines whether the means of two populations are equal; unlike the $t$-test we studied before for the same purpose, the Mann-Whitney U test can be applied when the populations are not normally distributed. The samples should be independent though, and the measurements should be identified by a factor variable that indicates the group to which an observation belongs.

*Demonstration Problem 17.1*: Mann-Whitney U Test, Small Samples

The challenge in applying this test in R is when the two groups (samples) are given separately and we need to put them together. If, on the other hand, the groups are already in the same file and each group is identified by an index (factor) variable, the `wilcox.test()` function can be applied without other preparations. Even in this case, though, make sure to declare the index variable as factor. The task in *Demonstration Problem 17.1* is to test whether health workers (`hw`) earn, on average, the same hourly wage as education workers (`ew`).

## 17.2. MANN–WHITNEY U TEST

```
hw<-c(20.1,19.8,22.36,18.75,21.9,22.96,20.75)
ew<-c(26.19,23.88,25.5,21.64,24.85,25.3,24.12,23.45)
lst<-list(H=hw,E=ew)
stk<-stack(lst)
wilcox.test(stk$values~stk$ind)
```

```
## 
##   Wilcoxon rank sum test
## 
## data:  stk$values by stk$ind
## W = 3, p-value = 0.002176
## alternative hypothesis: true location shift is not equal to 0
```

The low $p$-value indicates that there is a significant difference in earnings between the two categories of workers.

The next example concerns large samples, for which the R procedure is the same as for small samples. This example seeks to determine if the average incomes of families who view PBS television and families who do not view PBS television are equal.

```
pbs<-c(24500,39400,36800,43000,57960,32000,61000,34000,43500,
       55000,39000,62500,61400,53000)
npbs<-c(41000,32500,33000,21000,40500,32400,16000,21500,39500,
       27600,43500,51900,27800)
lst<-list(PBS=pbs,Non_PBS=npbs)
stk<-stack(lst)
wilcox.test(stk$values~stk$ind)
```

```
## 
##   Wilcoxon rank sum test with continuity correction
## 
## data:  stk$values by stk$ind
## W = 140.5, p-value = 0.0174
## alternative hypothesis: true location shift is not equal to 0
```

The warning about computing the $p$-value with ties refers to ties in the data, that is, when two or more values in the data set are equal, which makes the ranking not unique.

## 17.3 Wilcoxon Matched-Pairs Signed Rank Test

This is a nonparametric alternative to the $t$-test for related samples; it seeks to test the hypothesis that the two samples come from identical distributions; the test does not assume normality of the underlying populations.

$H_0$ : The samples come from identical distributions

$H_a$ : The samples come from different distributions

The R function is, as before, `wilcox.test()`, but with the argument paired=TRUE. The function `wilcox.test()` also accepts the type of the alternative hypothesis as an argument, which can be one of "less," "greater," or "two.sided." The following example is a small-sample case, which tests the hypothesis that the average household spending for healthcare is the same in Pittsburgh, Pennsylvania and Oakland, California, based on small samples of six families from each location. The families have been selected to be demographically similar.

```
pitt<-c(3750,3640,3815,3380,3590,3725)
oakl<-c(3560,3670,3610,3460,3140,3565)
lst<-list(P=pitt,O=oakl)
stk<-stack(lst)
wilcox.test(stk$values~stk$ind,paired=TRUE,alternative="two.sided")

##
##  Wilcoxon signed rank test
##
## data:  stk$values by stk$ind
## V = 18, p-value = 0.1563
## alternative hypothesis: true location shift is not equal to 0
```

Since the $p$-value is greater than 0.05, we cannot reject the null hypothesis that the two populations are identical, which means that the available data do not support the statement that Pittsburgh and Oakland have different healthcare spending patterns.

Let us apply the `wilcox.test()` function with paired data to a large sample example, to determine whether there is a difference in the cost per mile of airfares in the U.S. between two years, 1997 and 2016.

```
y97<-c(20.3,19.5,18.6,20.9,19.9,18.6,19.6,23.2,21.8,20.3,19.2,19.5,
       18.7,17.7,21.6,22.4,20.8)
y16<-c(22.8,12.7,14.1,16.1,25.2,20.2,14.9,21.3,18.7,20.9,22.6,16.9,
```

## 17.4. KRUSKAL–WALLIS TEST

```
            20.6,18.5,23.4,21.3,17.4)
lst<-list(y97=y97,y16=y16)
stk<-stack(lst)
wilcox.test(stk$values~stk$ind,paired=TRUE,alternative="two.sided")
```

```
##
##  Wilcoxon signed rank test with continuity correction
##
## data:  stk$values by stk$ind
## V = 98.5, p-value = 0.3087
## alternative hypothesis: true location shift is not equal to 0
```

## 17.4 Kruskal–Wallis Test

The test determines whether three or more samples come from the same populations, without the restrictive assumptions of the equivalent one-way ANOVA. For the Kruskal–Wallis test, the data is converted in rankings, and the test statistic is

$$K = \frac{12}{n(n+1)} \left( \sum_{j=1}^{c} \frac{T_j^2}{n_j} \right) - 3(n+1)$$

where:

- $c$ = total number of groups
- $n$ = total number of items
- $T_j$ = total ranks in group $j$
- $n_j$ = total number of items in group $j$
- $K \approx \chi^2$, with $df = c - 1$ if $n_j \geq 5$ for all $j$

Example: Determine if the number of patients seen in three types of offices are equal. The three types of offices are similar in all dimensions except for the number of partner physicians, with two physicians, three or more physicians, and an HMO office. The R function performing Kruskal-Wallis tests is `kruskal.test()`.

```
p2<-c(13,15,20,18,23)
p3<-c(24,16,19,22,25,14,17)
pHMO<-c(26,22,31,27,28,33)
lst<-list(p2,p3,pHMO)
kruskal.test(lst)
```

```
## 
##  Kruskal-Wallis rank sum test
## 
## data:  lst
## Kruskal-Wallis chi-squared = 9.571, df = 2, p-value = 0.00835
```

## 17.5 Friedman Test

This is a nonparametric alternative to the randomized block design, to be used when the normality assumption of the randomized block design is not possible or the researcher eals with ranked data. The Friedman test assumes that the blocks are independent from each other, that blocks are independent from treatment, and that observations within each block can be ranked. The test determines whether the treatment populations are identical, against the alternative than at least one is different.

The test procedure consists in converting all data to ranks and calculating the following test statistic:

$$\chi_r^2 = \frac{12}{bc(c+1)} \left( \sum_{j=1}^{c} R_j^2 \right) - 3b(c+1)$$

where

- $c$ = number of treatment levels (columns)
- $b$ = number of blocks (rows)
- $R_j$ = total number of ranks for a treatment level (column)
- $j$ = treatment level (column)
- $\chi_r^2 \approx \chi^2$, with $df = c - 1$

The R function performing a Friedman test is `friedman.test()`, which requires that the data is given as a matrix or a vector plus another vector of indexing.

*Demonstration Problem 17.5:* Brand Preference for Refrigerators

In this experiment, 10 potential customers are shown five brands of refrigerators (brands A, B, C, D, and E). The researcher asks the customers to rank each brand from 1 to 5 according to a customer's preference. We would like to determine whether there are significant differences between the rankings of these brands. In this example, the *treatment* is belonging to one of the brands, and a *block* is a customer.

To prepare the data for the function `friedman.test`, I will create a matrix using the five vectors of data, one for each brand.

## 17.6. SPEARMAN'S RANK CORRELATION

```
a<-c(3,1,3,2,5,1,4,2,2,3)
b<-c(5,3,4,3,4,5,1,3,4,5)
c<-c(2,2,5,1,2,3,3,4,5,4)
d<-c(4,4,2,4,1,4,2,5,3,2)
e<-c(1,5,1,5,3,2,5,1,1,1)
dat<-matrix(data=c(a,b,c,d,e),nrow=10,byrow=FALSE)
friedman.test(dat)

##
##  Friedman rank sum test
##
## data:  dat
## Friedman chi-squared = 3.68, df = 4, p-value = 0.451
```

The result of the test is not to reject the null hypothesis that the rankings are the same.

## 17.6 Spearman's Rank Correlation

This is a correlation measure that can be used to assess two variables are related when only rank data are available. If you recall, the Pearson $r$, which is an alternative to Spearman's rank correlation, requires at least interval data. Here is the formula for Spearman's rank correlation.

$$r_s = 1 - \frac{6 \sum d^2}{n(n^2 - 1)}$$

where:

- $n$ = number of pairs being correlated
- $d$ = the difference in the ranks of each pair

*Demonstration Problem 17.6*: Crude Oil vs. Gasoline Prices

The R function to calculate Spearman correlation is the same as for Pearson, namely cor(), with argument method="spearman".

```
poil<-c(14.6,10.5,12.3,15.10,18.35,22.6,28.9,31.4,26.75)
pgas<-c(3.25,3.26,3.28,3.26,3.32,3.44,3.56,3.60,3.54)
cor(poil,pgas,method="spearman")

## [1] 0.8954053
```

# Chapter 18

# Statistical Quality Control

## 18.1 Control Charts

The function qcc() in the R package qcc (Scrucca 2017) plots several types of control charts in R. The arguments of the function depend on the type of chart that you want to plot.

### The $\bar{x}$ Chart

An $\bar{x}$ chart shows the variation of the sample average over samples. Here is the code for constructing an $\bar{x}$ chart using the data in Problem 18.5; the chart is shown in Figure 18.1.

```
library(Black9edata)
library(qcc)
data(p18.5)
xbarChart<-qcc(p18.5,type="xbar",xlab="Sample",
  ylab="Average Weight (grams)",
  title=" ", add.stats=FALSE)
```

### The R Chart

The R chart shows the variation of the sample range for a number of given samples. The following example uses the data from Problem 18.5 in the textbook. The chart is shown in Figure 18.2.

```
library(qcc)
Rchart<-qcc(p18.5,type="R",xlab="Sample",ylab="Average Range",
            title=" ", add.stats=FALSE)
```

# CHAPTER 18. STATISTICAL QUALITY CONTROL

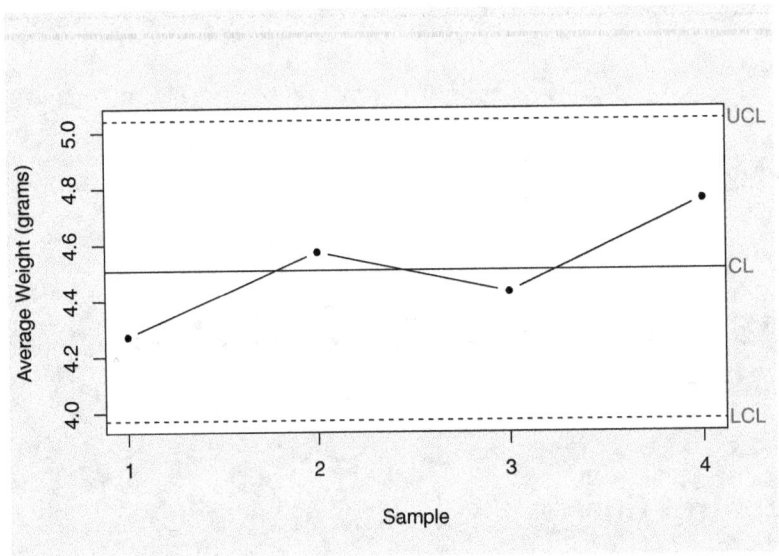

FIGURE 18.1 Average Weight for Whistles (x-Bar hart), Problem 18.5

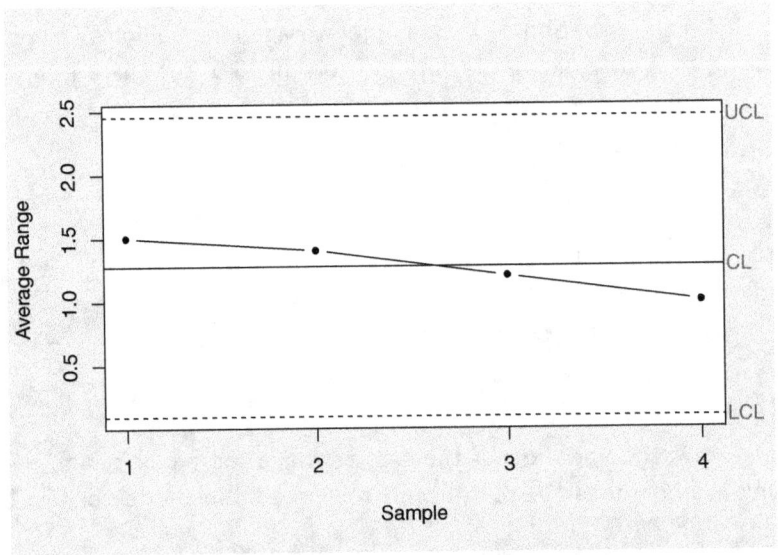

FIGURE 18.2 R-Chart for Problem 18.5

## 18.1. CONTROL CHARTS

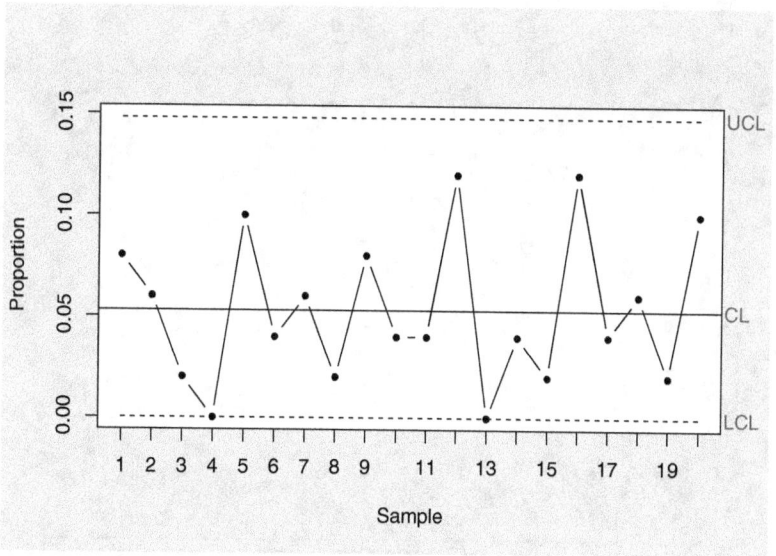

FIGURE 18.3 A p-Chart for Demonstration Problem 18.3

### The $p$ Chart

This chart presents the proportion of defective elements in each sample for a given number of samples. The function to be used for plotting such a chart is still qcc(), with type="p" and sizes= a vector containing the sample sizes. The next code lines construct a $p$ chart for the *Demonstration Problem 18.3*; Figure 18.3 shows the chart.

```
proportions<-c(4,3,1,0,5,2,3,1,4,2,2,6,0,2,1,6,2,3,1,5)
n=length(proportions)
s<-rep(50,n)
pChart<-qcc(proportions,type="p",sizes=s,
title=" ",xlab="Sample",ylab="Proportion", add.stats=FALSE)
```

### The $c$-Chart

A $c$-chart illustrates the number of defective characteristics per item. Figure 18.4 shows a $c$-chart for the *Demonstration Problem 18.4*.

```
defects<-c(2,0,3,1,2,5,3,2,0,0,4,3,2)
cchrt<-qcc(defects,type="c",xlab="Item",ylab="Defects",title=" ",
        add.stats=FALSE)
```

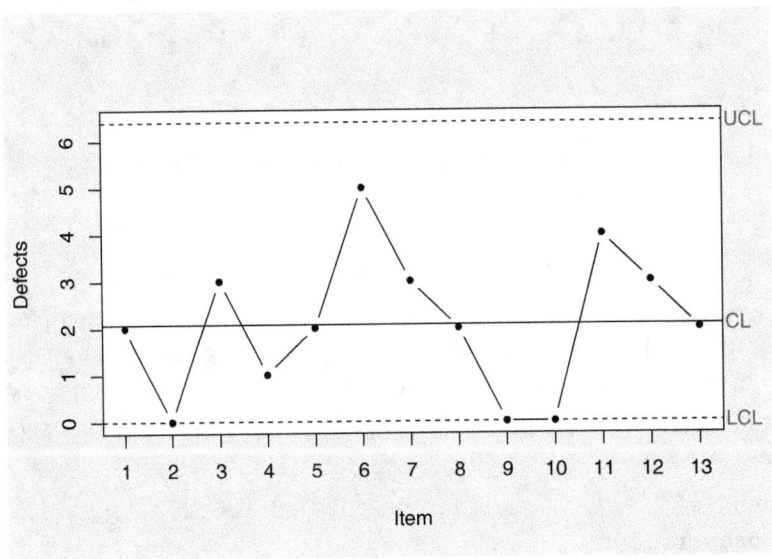

FIGURE 18.4 A c Chart for Demonstration Problem 18.4

# Chapter 19

# Decision Analysis

## 19.1 Decision Making Under Uncertainty

Consider a payoff matrix where each row corresponds to an available decision and each column corresponds to a possible, but uncertain, state of the world. The decision maker's task is to choose a decision under these circumstances; the outcome will depend, of course, on the criterion that the manager uses for decision making. (**Warning**: The codes in this chapter may not yield correct results in all situations. Please use them with care.)

**Maximax Criterion**

This is an optimistic decision maker's criterion; it assumes the best state of the world will occur, and chooses the decision that maximizes the payoff under this assumption. For each row, we identify the maximum payoff of all columns; then, we identify the row corresponding to the maximum of these maxima. The following code recognizes that the maximax criterion will always select the largest outcome in the payoff matrix. Thus, the code finds this maximum and returns its value together with its location in the matrix.

```
nrow<-4
ncol<-3
# Data should be introduced by columns
data<-c(-500,-100,300,-200,700,600,500,650,2200,900,750,1300)
dtable<-matrix(data,nrow=nrow,ncol=ncol)
```

```
MMloc<-which(dtable==max(dtable),arr.ind=TRUE)
MMvalue<-dtable[MMloc[1],MMloc[2]]
cat(" Maximax Criterion:","\n",
    " Payoff =",MMvalue,"\n",
    " Decision: ",MMloc[1],"\n",
    " State: ",MMloc[2])
```

```
##    Maximax Criterion:
##    Payoff = 2200
##    Decision:   1
##    State:   3
```

## Maximin Criterion

This criterion reflects a pessimistic view of the world: The decision maker assumes the worst will happen and tries to make the best decision under this assumption. Thus, the decision is the one that yields the highest payoff of the lowest possible under each available decision. The programming strategy is to form a vector of the lowest payoffs of each row (for each available decision) and then to pick the maximum of these. While it is easy to find this number, to identify its location is trickier. Yet we need to identify its position in the payoff matrix because the location reveals which decision should be adopted.

```
nrow<-4
ncol<-3
# The payoff matrix sould be introduced by columns
data<-c(-500,-100,300,-200,700,600,500,650,2200,900,750,1300)
dtable<-matrix(data,nrow=nrow,ncol=ncol)
Rm<-apply(dtable,1,min)#min of all states for each row
MmValue<-max(Rm)# the Maximin solution
row<-which(Rm==MmValue,arr.ind=TRUE)# the row of solution
col<-which(dtable[row,]==MmValue,arr.ind=TRUE)#col of solution
cat(" Maximin Criterion:","\n",
    " Payoff =",MmValue,"\n",
    " Decision: ",row,"\n",
    " State:",col)
```

```
##    Maximin Criterion:
##    Payoff = 300
```

## 19.1. DECISION MAKING UNDER UNCERTAINTY

```
##   Decision:  3
##   State: 1
```

### Hurwicz Criterion

The Hurwicz criterion chooses the decision that maximizes a weighted average between the worst and the best contingencies. The best contingency is weighted by the parameter $\alpha$, which, therefore, is a measure of the decision maker's optimism; the closer $\alpha$ is to 1, the more an optimistic choice is made.

```
nrow<-4
ncol<-3
# Data sould be introduced by columns
data<-c(-500,-100,300,-200,700,600,500,650,2200,900,750,1300)
alpha<-.7
dtable<-matrix(data,nrow=nrow,ncol=ncol)
Rm<-apply(dtable,1,min) #min of all states for each row
rM<-apply(dtable,1,max) #max of al states for each row
H<-(1-alpha)*Rm+alpha*rM #Hurwicz weighted average
row<-which(H==max(H),arr.ind=TRUE)
cat(" Hurwicz Criterion for alpha =",alpha,"\n",
    " Payoff =",H[row],"\n",
    " Decision: ",row)

##   Hurwicz Criterion for alpha = 0.7
##   Payoff = 1390
##   Decision:  1
```

### Minimax Regret Criterion

The minimax regret criterion creates, first, a loss table by subtracting each payoff in a state from the maximum payoff of that state. Then, the decision maker compares the maximum losses across states and chooses the decision corresponding to the least of them. Let us construct an R function to calculate the minimax regret choice. The mMreg() function requires the following arguments:

- data = the payoff matrix
- nrow = the number of decisions (number of rows int the matrix)
- ncol = the number of states (number of columns int the matrix)

```
#-----------------------------------------------------------------
#              Function: Minimax Regret Criterion
#-----------------------------------------------------------------
mMreg<-function(data,nrow,ncol){
  dtable<-matrix(data,nrow=nrow,ncol=ncol)
  cmax<-apply(dtable,2,max)
  maxmat<-matrix(rep(cmax,nrow),nrow,ncol,byrow=T)
  regmat<-maxmat-dtable
  MregVec<-apply(regmat,1,max)
  decision<-min(MregVec,arr.ind=TRUE)
  payoff<-min(MregVec)
  state<-which(regmat[decision,]==max(regmat[decision,])
          ,arr.ind=TRUE)
  lst<-c(Payoff=payoff,State=state,Decision=decision)
  return(lst)
  } #           End of Function
#-----------------------------------------------------------------
```

Now, apply the newly created mMreg() function to the investment example.

```
nrow<-4
ncol<-3
# Data should be introduced by columns
data<-c(-500,-100,300,-200,700,600,500,650,2200,900,750,1300)
mMreg(data,nrow,ncol)

##    Payoff   State Decision
##       800       1        1
```

## 19.2 Decision Making Under Risk

**Expected Monetary Value (EMV)**

This method requires a vector of probabilities, one probability for each state of the economy. Each column is multiplied by its corresponding probability; then, an expected payoff is determined for each state. The optimal decision is the one that maximizes the expected payoff across the states. The function EMV() built in the next code sequence

## 19.2. DECISION MAKING UNDER RISK

performs these calculations.

```
#-----------------------------------------------------------------
#              Function: Expected Monetary Value Criterion
#-----------------------------------------------------------------
EMV<-function(nrow,ncol,data,pVec){
  dtable<-matrix(data,nrow=nrow,ncol=ncol)
  eVec<-as.vector(dtable%*%pVec)# payoffs times probability vector
  decision<-which(eVec==max(eVec),arr.ind=TRUE)# the position of max
  maxpayoff<-max(eVec)
  lst<-c(Payoff=maxpayoff,Decision=decision)
  return(lst)
}#                                     End of Function
#-----------------------------------------------------------------
```

Here is the solution to the EMV investment example.

```
n<-4 # number of rows decisions) in the payoff matrix
m<-3 # number of columns (states) in the payoff matrix
# Data sould be introduced by columns
payoffs<-c(-500,-100,300,-200,700,600,500,650,2200,900,750,1300)
probabilities<-c(.25,.45,.3)
EMV(n,m,payoffs,probabilities)
```

```
##   Payoff Decision
##      850        1
```

*Demonstration Problem 19.2:* Expected Monetary Value

Find the EMV and recommend a decision for the given payoff table.

```
payoffs<-c(-3,-40,-210,2,-28,-145,3,10,-5,6,20,55)
probabilities<-c(.1,.25,.4,.25)
decisions<-3
states<-4
EMV(decisions,states,payoffs,probabilities)
```

```
##   Payoff Decision
```

## 2.9 1.0

**Expected Value of Perfect Information**

The expected value of perfect information is equal to the difference between the payoff when the state of the world is known and the payoff when the state of the world is unknown. This puts a monetary value on information and allows deciding how much to spend to acquire that information.

```
#-----------------------------------------------------------------
#          Function: Expected Value of Perfect Information
#-----------------------------------------------------------------
EVPI<-function(nrow,ncol,data,pVec){
  dtable<-matrix(data,nrow=nrow,ncol=ncol)
  eVec<-as.vector(dtable%*%pVec) # payoffs times probability vector
  EMVI<-max(eVec)
  Mcol<-t(as.vector(apply(dtable,2,max))) # max for each state
  EMPPI<-as.numeric(Mcol%*%pVec)
  VPI<-EMPPI-EMVI
  lst<-c(EVPI=VPI)
  return(lst)
}#                               End of Function
#-----------------------------------------------------------------
```

Application of the EVPI() function to the investment example:

```
n<-4
m<-3
# Data sould be introduced by columns
data<-c(-500,-100,300,-200,700,600,500,650,2200,900,750,1300)
probabilities<-c(.25,.45,.3)
EVPI(n,m,data,probabilities)
```

## EVPI
## 200

## 19.3 Revising Probabilities

The next function to construct is more involved than the previous ones; it seeks to solve a decision tree with revised probabilities. Thus, it requires, besides the payoff matrix and its (prior) state probabilities, an $m \times m$ matrix of probabilities that reflects the accuracy of forecasts for each state. The rows in this matrix are forecasts of the states, while the columns are the states themselves. Thus, entry $[i,j]$ in this matrix is the conditional probability of forecasting state $i$ given that state $j$ occurs. The sum of these probabilities has to be 1 for each column, but not for each row. I denoted this matrix by fs in the bayesTree() function; in addition, I denoted by sf the revised probabilities, which form an $m \times m$ matrix of conditional probabilities that state $i$ occurs when state $j$ was forecasted.

```
#-----------------------------------------------------------------
#                  Function: Bayes Tree
#-----------------------------------------------------------------
bayesTree<-function(data,n,m,s,fs){
  P<-matrix(data,nrow=n,ncol=m)
  fs<-matrix(fs,nrow=m,ncol=m)   # P(f_i/s_j)
  f<-as.vector(fs%*%s)           # P(f_j)
  sf<-matrix(rep(0,m*m),nrow=m,ncol=m) #P(s_i/f_j)
  for(i in 1:m){
    for(j in 1:m){
    sf[i,j]=fs[j,i]*s[i]/f[j]   #Revised probabilities
    }
  }
  r1<-matrix(0,m,n)
  for (i in 1:m){          # forecast
    for(j in 1:n){         # decision
    r1[i,j]<-sum(P[j,]*sf[,i]) #expected payoffs stage 1
    }
  }
  r1max<-apply(r1,1,max) #choose max of each state stage 1
  r<-as.numeric(t(r1max)%*%f)
  lst<-c(Payoff=r)
  return(lst)
}#              End of Function
#-----------------------------------------------------------------
```

Here is an application of the revised probabilities method:

```
n<-2 # number of rows (decisions) in the payoff matrix
m<-2 # number of columns (states) in the payoff matrix
# Data must be introduced by columns
data<-c(500,-200,100,1100)
s<-c(.65,.35)# Prior probabilities of states
fs<-c(.8,.2,.3,.7)# forecast success rates by columns
bayesTree(data,n,m,s,fs)

## Payoff
##     514
```

*Example*: Problem 19.13

```
data=c(-225,125,350,425,-150,-400)
n=3
m=2
s<-c(.6,.4)
fs<-c(.75,.25,.15,.85)
emvP<-EMV(n,m,data,s)[[1]]
BayP<-bayesTree(data,n,m,s,fs)
vInf<-BayP-emvP
cat("   EMV Payoff =",emvP,"\n",
    " Revised Probabilities Payoff =",BayP,"\n",
    " Value of Information =",vInf)

##     EMV Payoff = 50
##     Revised Probabilities Payoff = 244.25
##     Value of Information = 194.25
```

The decision maker should purchase information if its price is less than $194.25.

*Demonstration Problem 19.4:* The Value of Information

```
data=c(-3,-50,2,-20,6,65)
n=2
m=3
s<-c(.2,.3,.5)
fs<-c(.75,.2,.05,.1,.8,.1,.05,.3,.65)
emvP<-EMV(n,m,data,s)[[1]]
BayP<-bayesTree(data,n,m,s,fs)
```

## 19.3. REVISING PROBABILITIES

```
vInf=BayP-emvP
cat(" EMV Payoff =",emvP,"\n",
    " Revised Probabilities Payoff =",BayP,"\n",
    " Value of Information =",vInf)

##    EMV Payoff = 16.5
##    Revised Probabilities Payoff = 22.735
##    Value of Information = 6.235
```

The decision maker should buy the information only if its price is less than $6.235.

# References

Black, Ken. 2017. *Business Statistics for Contemporary Decision Making*. http://ca.wiley.com/WileyCDA/WileyTitle/productCd-1119320895,subjectCd-BA04.html.

Colonescu, Constantin. 2016. *Black9edata: Business Statistics R Data*.

Fox, John, and Sanford Weisberg. 2017. *Car: Companion to Applied Regression*. https://CRAN.R-project.org/package=car.

R Core Team. 2017. *R: A Language and Environment for Statistical Computing*. Vienna, Austria: R Foundation for Statistical Computing. https://www.R-project.org/.

RStudio Team. 2015. *RStudio: Integrated Development Environment for R*. Boston, MA: RStudio, Inc. http://www.rstudio.com/.

Scrucca, Luca. 2017. *Qcc: Quality Control Charts*. https://CRAN.R-project.org/package=qcc.

Williams, Ken. 2011. *Function to Calculate Mode*. stackoverflow. goo.gl/5TBuR0.

Xie, Yihui. 2017. *Bookdown: Authoring Books and Technical Documents with R Markdown*. Boca Raton, FL: Chapman; Hall/CRC. https://github.com/rstudio/bookdown.

www.ingramcontent.com/pod-product-compliance
Lightning Source LLC
Chambersburg PA
CBHW081017240526
45471CB00017B/3190